Praise for *Th*

"That power is not taken but given is true for most human relations today. It has ancient roots in primate behavior. Dacher Keltner applies a lifetime of research to this topic, offering a lively description of how true power is like a return on a social investment in others."

—Frans de Waal, author of *Are We Smart Enough to Know How Smart Animals Are?*

"Dacher Keltner is the most interesting psychologist in America. He's busy changing the minds of Americans about how power works, how inequality works. It's only a matter of time before his ideas spread everywhere. And unlike most psychologists I know, he's not a weirdo."

—Michael Lewis, author of *The Big Short* and *Moneyball*

"An innovative look at the idea of power . . . [This] paradigm-shifting book challenges readers to find a new level of awareness about themselves and the leaders they choose to follow."

—*Publishers Weekly*

"*The Power Paradox*, compelling and eye-opening from start to finish, will change your view of what power is. Power turns out to be a subtler force than it seems, influencing us for better and worse more than we realize. This book explains how people get power, keep it, and keep from being corrupted by it. The good news is the radical claim at the heart of the book: that the best way to get and keep power is to use it for the greater good. This pathbreaking book is full of fascinating and little-known findings, and Dacher Keltner's many years of creative work on the psychology of status and influence make him uniquely qualified to write it."

—Robert Wright, author of *The Evolution of God* and *The Moral Animal*

"Dacher Keltner shares insights into many aspects of power, including afternoon tea in Britain and how Lincoln won the presidency. His combination of academic sophistication and clear style delivers a new concept of power in our society today that is provocative and intriguing."
  —Sheryl WuDunn, coauthor of *Half the Sky* and *A Path Appears*

"With personal insight and the latest science, Dacher Keltner is both realistic and idealistic: *The Power Paradox* sheds light on human power's dark side, as well as its redeeming qualities. Everyone can learn from this wise book."
  —Susan T. Fiske, Eugene Higgins Professor of Psychology and Professor of Public Affairs at Princeton University

"*The Power Paradox* brings clarity to our confusion, brimming with evidence-based insights into powerlessness, the selfish uses of power, and the best kind: power that furthers the greater good. Dacher Keltner's brilliant research gives us a lens that lets us see afresh hidden patterns in society, politics, and our own lives. No doubt this will be one of the most significant science books of the decades."
  —Daniel Goleman, author of *Emotional Intelligence* and *A Force for Good: The Dalai Lama's Vision for Our World*

PENGUIN BOOKS

THE POWER PARADOX

Dacher Keltner is a professor of psychology at the University of California, Berkeley, and the faculty director of UC Berkeley's Greater Good Science Center. A renowned expert in the science of human emotion, Dr. Keltner studies compassion and awe, how we express emotion, and how emotions guide our moral identities and search for meaning. His research interests also span issues of power, status, inequality, and social class. He is the author of *The Power Paradox*, the bestselling books *Born to Be Good* and *Awe*, and the coeditor of *The Compassionate Instinct*.

THE POWER
PARADOX

How We Gain and Lose Influence

Dacher Keltner

PENGUIN BOOKS

PENGUIN BOOKS
An imprint of Penguin Random House LLC
375 Hudson Street
New York, New York 10014
penguin.com

First published in the United States of America by Penguin Press,
an imprint of Penguin Random House LLC, 2016
Published in Penguin Books 2017

Illustration credits appear on pages 195–96.

ISBN 9780143110293 (paperback)
ISBN 9781594205248 (hardcover)
ISBN 9780698195592 (ebook)
ISBN 9780735221284 (international edition)

Printed in the United States of America

DESIGNED BY AMANDA DEWEY

To my team at the Berkeley Social Interaction Lab.
Without you, I would never have been able to tell this story.

Contents

INTRODUCTION   *1*

One
POWER IS ABOUT MAKING A
DIFFERENCE IN THE WORLD   *19*

Two
POWER IS GIVEN, NOT GRABBED   *41*

Three
ENDURING POWER COMES FROM
A FOCUS ON OTHERS   *69*

Four
THE ABUSES OF POWER   *99*

Five

THE PRICE OF POWERLESSNESS *137*

Epilogue

A FIVEFOLD PATH TO POWER *159*

Acknowledgments *165*

Notes *167*

Index *187*

THE POWER PARADOX

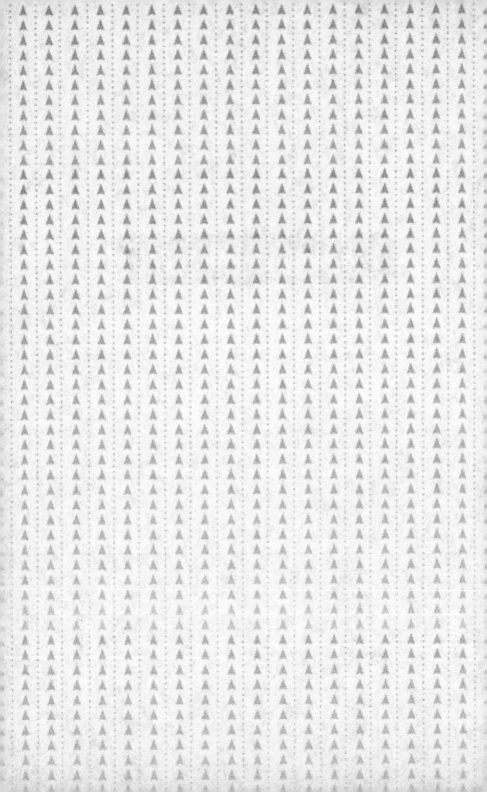

Introduction

Life is made up of patterns. Patterns of eating, thirst, sleep, and fight-or-flight are crucial to our individual survival; patterns of courtship, sex, attachment, conflict, play, creativity, family life, and collaboration are crucial to our collective survival. Wisdom is our ability to perceive these patterns and to shape them into coherent chapters within the longer narrative of our lives.

This book is about a pattern of social living that makes up our daily interactions and shapes what our lives will, in the end, amount to. It has profound implications for whether you will have a sexual affair, break the law, suffer from panic attacks, be leveled by depression, die early due to a chronic illness, or find purpose in life and bring it to fruition. This pattern kept appearing in scientific studies I've conducted over these past twenty years. It's called the power paradox.

The power paradox is this: we rise in power and make a difference in the world due to what is best about human nature, but we fall from power due to what is worst. We gain a capacity to make a difference in the world by enhancing the lives of others, but the very experience of having power and privilege leads us to behave, in our worst moments, like impulsive, out-of-control sociopaths.

How we handle the power paradox guides our personal and work lives and determines, ultimately, how happy we and the people we care about will be. It determines our empathy, generosity, civility, innovation, intellectual rigor, and the collaborative strength of our communities and social networks. Its ripple effects shape the patterns that make up our families, neighborhoods, and workplaces, as well as the broader patterns of social organization that define societies and our current political struggles: sexual violence; bias and discrimination against blacks, Asians, Latinos, and gays; and systemic poverty and inequality. Handling the power paradox well is fundamental to the health of our society.

Twenty years ago, when I began the studies that uncovered the power paradox, I confronted the question: what is power? To outsmart the power paradox, we need to know what power is. The first surprise that my scientific inquiry produced was this: our culture's understanding of power has been deeply and enduringly shaped by one person—Niccolò Machiavelli—and his powerful sixteenth-century book *The Prince.* In that book the Florentine author argued that power is, in its essence, about force, fraud, ruthlessness, and strategic violence. Following Machiavelli, the widespread tendency has been to think of power as involving extraordinary acts of coercive force. Power was what the great dictators wielded; power was embodied in generals making decisive moves on battlefields, businessmen initiating hostile takeovers, coworkers sacrificing colleagues to advance their own careers, and bullies on the middle-school playground tormenting smaller kids.

But this view of power fails upon careful scrutiny today. It cannot make sense of many important changes in human history: the abolition of slavery, the toppling of dictators, the ending of apartheid, and the rise of the civil rights, women's rights, and gay rights movements, to name just a few. It cannot make sense of the great social changes brought about by medical advances, social media, new laws protecting the less powerful, great films, the birth control pill, radical paintings and novels, and scientific discoveries. Perhaps most critically, thinking of power as coercive force and fraud blinds us to its pervasiveness in our daily lives and the fact that it shapes our every interaction, from those between parents and children to those between work colleagues.

POWER IS ABOUT MAKING A DIFFERENCE IN THE WORLD

Society has changed dramatically since Machiavelli's Renaissance Florence in ways that require us to move beyond outdated notions of power. We will be more poised to outsmart the power paradox if we broaden our thinking and define power as the capacity to make a difference in the world, in particular by stirring others in our social networks.

This new definition of power reveals that it is not something limited to rare individuals in dramatic moments of their highly visible lives—to malevolent dictators, high-profile politicians, or the jet-setting rich and famous; nor does it exist solely in boardrooms, on battlefields, or on the U.S. Senate floor. Instead, power defines the waking life of every human being. It is found not only in extraordinary acts but also in quotidian acts, indeed in every interaction and every relationship, be it an attempt to get a two-year-old to eat green vegetables or to inspire a stubborn colleague to do her best work. It lies in providing an opportunity to someone, or asking a friend the right question to stir creative thought, or calming a colleague's rattled nerves, or directing resources to a young person trying to make it in society. Power dynamics, patterns of mutual influence, define the ongoing interactions between fetus and mother, infant and parent, between romantic partners, childhood friends, teens, people at work, and groups in conflict. Power is the medium through which we relate to one another. Power is about making a difference in the world by influencing others.

POWER IS GIVEN TO US BY OTHERS

How do we gain power—the capacity to make a difference in the world? The old Machiavellian philosophy of power treated it as something that is grabbed. Narratives of power grabs make for great literature and art—*Macbeth*, *Julius Caesar*, *The Godfather*, and, more recently, *House of Cards*. It is captivating to read about cunning acts of manipulation and the bloody elimination of rivals and allies. But they are more the stuff of fiction and the past than about how people enact power in the twenty-first century.

Instead, a new wave of thinking about power reveals that it is given to us by others rather than grabbed. We gain power by acting in ways that improve the lives of other people in our social networks. Our power is granted to us by others. This is true at work, in social organizations of different kinds, and in our friendships, romantic partnerships, and families.

In one of the central developments of hominid evolution, vertical hierarchies (seen today among our primate relatives, the great apes) gave way to more horizontal patterns of social organization. The hunter-gatherers who are still around today live in the small groups that were typical of the conditions of human evolution. Within these conditions, we became a hypersocial species, raising profoundly vulnerable offspring, gathering food, creating shelter, and defending ourselves collaboratively and in small groups. Hierarchies were still present as we evolved, but given our hypersociality, individuals could band together in patterns of alliances and readily constrain those who might abuse power. As a result, groups gained the capacity to grant power to those who advanced the greater good rather than to coercive, forceful Machiavellians.

Groups give power continually to individuals in patterns of social behavior that often mystify or are objects of scorn and derision. Like it or not, our species is reputation mad—just look at the astonishing growth of Facebook, the enduring fascination with the gossipy characters in Jane Austen novels, and industries that have sprouted up around the burnishing of reputations. The pursuit of a good reputation is central to social life. We may exhort young people to not worry about their reputations, to privilege authentic self-expression no matter what others think. But groups construct reputations of individuals to mark their capacity for power and to provide a check against its potential abuse. Your power is only as good as your reputation.

Your reputation arises in patterns of communication within groups, and in particular through gossip. Far from being idle, inconsequential, or easily rooted out of social life, gossip is the sophisticated means by which group members spread information that feeds into reputations. Using gossip, a group can track an individual's likelihood of advancing its interests and determine what power each individual has.

Groups also empower individuals through status-enhancing esteem, a social reward that motivates behavior as powerfully as does the desire for sex or cravings for chocolate. In strategically giving esteem to individuals, groups encourage those with power to continue to act in ways that are good for the group, making it feel good to do good. Our influence, the lasting difference that we make in the world, is ultimately only as good as what others think of us. Having enduring power is a privilege that depends on other people continuing to give it to us.

We have arrived at the pivotal moment in the power paradox: what *you* do with power. Will you continue to make a difference in the world and enjoy the lasting esteem of others? Or will you lose your power, as so many before you have done? What are the practices that determine keeping or losing power?

Outside of falling in love, there may be no more widely considered pattern to social life than the rise to power, the abuse of power, and the subsequent fall from power. We are transfixed by the falls from power that follow its abuse. Think of President

Richard Nixon's resignation, the statue of Saddam Hussein being toppled after the "shock and awe" campaign (a campaign that in itself was a fall from power for the United States), the collapse of Enron, or Michael Milken, Martha Stewart, Dennis Kozlowski, and Bernie Madoff doing prison time. Our fixation on the fall from power leads us to believe that the abuse of power is inevitable. But the power paradox is more complex than that. Thankfully, a bit more choice is involved. It is not human nature to abuse power. To understand how this is so, we need to understand what power does to how we perceive the world.

Power is not only the capacity to influence others; it is also a state of mind. The feeling of having power is a rush of expectancy, delight, and confidence, giving us a sense of agency and, ultimately, purpose. Throughout the world people experience power as the vital force guiding their lives. Power is a dopamine high, and these initial feelings can spiral into ways of interacting with others that resemble a manic episode. (And yes, bouts of mania are associated with elevated feelings of power.)

Every time we experience power—a recurrent feeling in our everyday interactions—we find ourselves at a moment, a fork in the road, where we must confront perhaps the most important choice we will make in life, yet one we make on a daily basis. Propelled forward by the feeling of power, we can act in ways that lead us to enjoy enduring power, have lasting influence in the world, and continue to be esteemed by others, or we can be seduced by the self-indulgent possibilities that power occasions. Which path you take matters enormously.

POWER IS GAINED AND MAINTAINED THROUGH A FOCUS ON OTHERS

Handling the power paradox depends on finding a balance between the gratification of your own desires and your focus on other people. As the most social of species, we evolved several other-focused, universal social practices that bring out the good in others and that make for strong social collectives. A thoughtful practitioner of these practices will not be misled by the rush of the experience of power down the path of self-gratification and abuse, but will choose instead to enjoy the deeper delights of making a lasting difference in the world. These social practices are fourfold: empathizing, giving, expressing gratitude, and telling stories. All four of these practices dignify and delight others. They constitute the basis of strong, mutually empowered ties. You can lean on them to enhance your power at any moment of the day by stirring others to effective action.

THE ABUSES OF POWER

Straying from an intent focus upon others can catapult you toward selfish and shortsighted behavior, the kind of abuses of power that fill the pages of our daily newspapers, history books, biographies, and the works of Shakespeare and many other great authors.

It isn't just the wealthy and famous who can be undone by

the seductions of power; it's any one of us at any moment. To lose focus on others can lead to empathy deficits and the loss of compassion, impulsive and unethical action, and rude and uncivil behavior. When we are feeling powerful, we can easily rationalize our unethical actions with stories of our own superiority, which demean others.

This is the heart of the power paradox: the seductions of power induce us to lose the very skills that enabled us to gain power in the first place. Abuses of power occur in every corner of our social life—and lead to greedy eating, swearing, rudeness, lying, sexual affairs, sexual violence, racial violence, unethical behavior, and arrogant driving. By succumbing to the power paradox, we undermine our own power and cause others, on whom our power so critically depends, to feel threatened and devalued. Cumulative abuses of power lead to diminished trust at work, reduced commitment and closeness in families, and the unraveling of the cooperative fabric of civil society.

THE PRICE OF POWERLESSNESS

Today poverty affects one in seven of all Americans. An astonishing proportion of American children are hungry, sick, and unable to concentrate in school. For thirty years economic inequality has expanded, to the point that the ever-widening gap between rich and poor is generally considered to be the most pernicious social problem facing the United States.

United States politics is almost exclusively run by the very wealthy, who, succumbing to the power paradox, may be the very people most blind to the problems of powerlessness, poverty, and inequality. As economic inequality expands in the United States, poverty and racism are persistent. The deaths of Michael Brown, Eric Garner, Freddie Gray, and many unseen others, followed by the Black Lives Matter movement, have prompted acute concerns about coercive institutional force. Social institutions—social clubs, prep schools, elite private colleges, cotillions, fraternities and sororities, and charity and corporate boards—perpetuate, to some degree inadvertently and to some degree intentionally, power imbalances.

Missing from our conversation about these social issues is the psychology of powerlessness. How, as the scientists at the heart of this new line of inquiry like to say, does powerlessness—resulting from poverty, inequality, racism, gender bias—"get under our skin"? Economic inequality within cities, counties, states, and nations leads to a lack of trust, impulsive behavior, a diminished sense of community, poor health, depression, anxiety, and violence. The costs of powerlessness, which are so often the result of others succumbing to the power paradox, are profound. Powerlessness amplifies the individual's sensitivity to threat; it hyperactivates the stress response and the hormone cortisol; and it damages the brain. These effects compromise our ability to reason, to reflect, to engage in the world, and to feel good and hopeful about the future. Powerlessness, I believe, is the greatest threat outside of climate change facing our society today.

THE NEW SCIENCE OF POWER

A critical task of science is to provide clear nomenclature—precise terms that sharpen our understanding of patterned phenomena in the outside world and inside the mind. This is especially necessary when it comes to discussions of power, a word that can refer to so many different things—money, fame, social class, respect, physical strength, energy, political participation. As a social psychologist, my focus is on what power does to our personal and social lives, and how our power arises during the social interactions that make up our daily lives.

Here are a few definitions that derive from this focus and that will be critical to appreciating the power principles that a new science of power has discovered.

POWER your capacity to make a difference in the world by influencing the states of other people.

STATUS the respect that you enjoy from other people in your social network; the esteem they direct to you. Status goes with power often but not always.

CONTROL your capacity to determine the outcomes in your life. You can have complete control over your life—think of the reclusive hermit—but have no power.

SOCIAL CLASS the mixture of family wealth, educational achievement, and occupational prestige that you enjoy; alternatively, the subjective sense you have of where you stand on a class ladder in society, high, middle, or low. Both forms of social class are societal forms of power.

As we move through the new science of power, we shall see how these different forms of rank relate to one another and often shape our behavior according to the principles it has uncovered.

Equipped with these definitions, we are poised to embark on a tour of the new science of power. Before doing so, I should make clear that this book is *not* about leadership per se, about inspirational leaders today or in history, or about people who abuse their power; many books already fit this bill. I do teach leaders of all kinds, in business, science, education, government, philanthropy, technology, health care, biotech, and finance. They know firsthand that the power paradox is relevant to their work and that outsmarting it is critical to great and enduring leadership. They have seen how the abuses of power can undermine organizations and people's lives.

I also have also spent a lot of time with people who lead really successful teams at Facebook, Pixar, and Google, and with inmates leading restorative justice programs in San Quentin State Prison. I have seen leaders embody many of the twenty power principles that you'll learn of in this book. (I've listed those principles on pages 16–17.) But I'm not the person to do the in-depth reporting on groundbreaking visionaries for a book on leadership.

This book is also *not* about politics. After I speak to audiences, I often get political and historical questions. This is sensible, for we often equate power with politics. What about Hitler? ISIS? Doesn't this explain everything about Robespierre and the French Revolution? What would the country be like if Sheryl Sandberg were president? I don't know, and I usually embarrass myself when I offer up a half-baked idea as an answer. But knowing about the power paradox can help us understand, for example, Stalin's campaign of terror, Kennedy's disastrous Bay of Pigs invasion, why one candidate appeals more than another to the body politic, the role of journalism in holding the powerful accountable, why trickle-down economics does not rest upon a realistic understanding of the psychological effects of wealth, the problems of American politics, and how massive acts of ruthless force ("shock and awe," Vietnam) can backfire and cost a nation in terms of its power.

I do believe the twenty power principles—which are about face-to-face power dynamics in social groups—illuminate not only falls from power and the enduring legacies of politicians but also power dynamics at different levels of political analysis—the fate of political parties and ideological movements, and why nations rise and fall in similar ways across history. The principles are relevant to serious debates taking place right now about the shifting power of nations, about "soft power" and "hard power" on the international stage, and about the surprising and lasting influence of soft power (culture, ideas, art, and institutions) as compared to hard power (military might, invasion, and economic sanctions). But the in-depth, historically situated, highly contextual analysis of national and international politics is better left for people who are steeped in the methods and wisdom of those traditions—historians, political scientists, cultural critics, and journalists, to name a few. You might think of this book as an examination of power for every person.

We live in perhaps the most dynamic moment in human history when it comes to power. Women are assuming unprecedented power (although they are still not paid fair wages and are still underrepresented in positions of leadership, for example as CEOs). New economic superpowers—India and China—have arrived, raising complex and necessary questions about the nature of American power. Old superpowers led by apparent Machiavellians—such as Russia—are waking up. Organizations are moving from vertical to more horizontal structures (although dramatic pay inequalities persist). Facebook, Google, Twitter, Instagram, Snapchat, and Tumblr have radically changed how ideas flow through networks, the extent to which others know our actions, and the very nature of human influence. At the same time, state-based, coercive power persists, as is evident in the flurry of documented police brutality. We need to think of power in a new way and be steadfast in our efforts to outsmart the power paradox.

We can understand ourselves only through the lens of power. Much of what we delight about in our social lives is irreducibly about how we handle the power paradox—forming friendships, finding contentment with family members, ensuring the long-term quality of our romantic lives, making contributions in our work lives, engaging in our communities, and enjoying the social delights of the quotidian life—gossiping, sharing, touching, expressing gratitude, having sex, telling stories, teasing, sleeping, eating, and maintaining our health. And much of what is most unsettling about human nature—stigma, greed, arrogance, racial and sexual violence, and the nonrandom distribution of depression and bad health to the poor—follows from how we handle the power paradox. I hope that in reading this book, you will learn in your own particular ways how to transcend the power paradox and to find delight in making a difference in the world.

POWER PRINCIPLES ▶

PRINCIPLE #1

Power is about altering the states of others.

PRINCIPLE #2

Power is part of every relationship and interaction.

PRINCIPLE #3

Power is found in everyday actions.

PRINCIPLE #4

Power comes from empowering others in social networks.

PRINCIPLE #5

Groups give power to those who advance the greater good.

PRINCIPLE #6

Groups construct reputations that determine the capacity to influence.

PRINCIPLE #7

Groups reward those who advance the greater good with status and esteem.

PRINCIPLE #8

Groups punish those who undermine the greater good with gossip.

PRINCIPLE #9

Enduring power comes from empathy.

PRINCIPLE #10

Enduring power comes from giving.

PRINCIPLE #11

Enduring power comes from expressing gratitude.

PRINCIPLE #12

Enduring power comes from telling stories that unite.

PRINCIPLE #13

Power leads to empathy deficits and diminished moral sentiments.

PRINCIPLE #14

Power leads to self-serving impulsivity.

PRINCIPLE #15

Power leads to incivility and disrespect.

PRINCIPLE #16

Power leads to narratives of exceptionalism.

PRINCIPLE #17

Powerlessness involves facing environments of continual threat.

PRINCIPLE #18

Stress defines the experience of powerlessness.

PRINCIPLE #19

Powerlessness undermines the ability to contribute to society.

PRINCIPLE #20

Powerlessness causes poor health.

Power Is About Making a Difference in the World

When I began my study of power twenty years ago, power was often equated with coercion, might, and dominance. The rise and fall of nations was explained in terms of military innovation, conquest, and overreach and the effects of martial activities upon a country's economic strength. Class relations were described in terms of the oppressor and the oppressed and in terms of how economic domination determines the contents of consciousness. Gender relations were seen through the lens of subjugation.

This view of power as coercion finds its clearest expression in Niccolò Machiavelli's *The Prince*, which is read by hundreds of thousands of students in history courses every year and is taught in schools of government, business, and public policy around the world. Machiavelli wrote during a time of extreme violence.

Murder was about one hundred times more common than it is today. Rape was acceptable. Torture was a public spectacle often accompanied by song and poetry. Abuses of power could largely go unchecked: few people could read, there was no journalism to hold the powerful accountable, there was no organized militia to institutionalize martial force, and there was little notion of universal individual rights.

The Prince offers a philosophy of power suitable to such violent times, treating power in its purest form as "force and fraud." We gain and keep such power by committing coercive and unpredictable acts that are impetuous, fierce, and violent. We hold on to such power by appearing virtuous even though we harbor other intentions. This kind of power quiets (or kills) rivals and critics, inspires allegiances, and mutes the masses. Through coercive force and fraud, we dominate.

But counterexamples to this conception of power readily come to mind. Many of the most significant changes in our history—the adoption of women's suffrage, civil rights legislation, the free speech movement and its influence upon the protests against the Vietnam War, the overthrow of apartheid, the rise of gay rights—were brought about by people who lacked economic, political, and military might; they changed the world without coercive force.

One recent study examined 323 opposition movements from 1900 to 2006, in places ranging from East Timor to countries of the former Soviet bloc. Some of these movements used the tactics of coercive force—bombs, assassinations, beheadings, torture, and civilian killings. Others relied on nonviolent tactics—marches, vigils, petitions, and boycotts. The latter were twice as likely

(53 percent versus 26 percent) to lead to achieving gains in political power, winning broad support from citizens, and contributing to the fall of oppressive regimes.

People resort to coercive force when their power is actually slipping. In our professional lives, people who endorse Machiavellian strategies to social life—lying, manipulating, and stepping on others to rise in the ranks—actually report experiencing less power and influence than the average person. In our personal lives, romantic partners are more likely to treat their beloved in coercive ways—through bullying, physical abuse, and emotional threats—when they are feeling *less* powerful. Parents are vulnerable to abusing their children when they feel relatively *powerless* vis-à-vis a willful child. In schools, bullies are continually engaging in domineering and deceptive actions, but they typically rank near the bottom of their class in status, respect, and influence in their peers' eyes. Today coercive force is a more likely path to powerlessness than to gains in power.

The Machiavellian lens blinds us to the pervasiveness of power in our daily lives. When we equate power to the ruthless violence of notorious dictators—Hitler, Stalin, Saddam Hussein, Pol Pot—we will fail to appreciate how power shapes our own interactions with our friends, parents, romantic partners, children, and work colleagues. When we think of power in terms of extraordinary acts of domination—tanks rolling through villages, guards treating naked prisoners like dogs at Abu Ghraib—we will fail to understand how power shapes more ordinary acts of creativity, reasoning, ethical judgment, affection, and emotion. Conceptualizing power as coercion impedes our attempt to grapple with the power paradox because it distorts our very understanding of what power is.

In 1938, with Fascism taking hold in Europe, the English philosopher Bertrand Russell observed that "the fundamental concept in social science is Power, in the same sense that Energy is the fundamental concept in physics. . . . The laws of social dynamics are laws which can only be stated in terms of power."

Our challenge is to understand how all social dynamics are shaped by power. The past forty years have seen a shift away from coercive force as the basis and expression of power. Forty years ago people believed that leadership required dominance, assertiveness, and force, whether it was in business, law, journalism, politics, sports, or community organizations. But today things are different, reflecting the social changes of the recent past: in North America, South America, Europe, Asia, and the Middle East, people have come to believe that power is best expressed in compassion and enhancing the well-being of others, and that warmth and understanding are just as important to strong leadership as forceful, assertive, and bold behavior.

A first step in meeting Bertrand Russell's challenge, then, is to broaden our thinking about what power is. A new conceptualization of power should apply to all relationships and interactions of every kind, not just to those involving asymmetrical force. It should illuminate the myriad ways we influence one another: by stimulating new ideas, leading protests, lifting up those in need, or redirecting the flow of capital. It should apply to all the contexts in which humans interact and help us understand all forms of social change.

Here is a definition that meets these requirements: power is about making a difference in the world. This definition at its core is pragmatic: power is about changing other people's lives. The definition reflects our highly social nature: we make a difference in the world by influencing other people.

This definition challenges certain misconceptions. Power is not necessarily about attention or fame, for the famous often do little to make a difference in the world, while those who do bring about change typically remain unknown, experiencing little fame. Nor is power necessarily about wealth or social class, as is so often assumed. People's social class—the combination of their wealth, education, and occupational prestige—accounts for only 10 to 15 percent of how powerful and influential they feel at any moment. Money and class translate to power only when people use these resources to make a difference in others' lives.

If we grant that power is about making a difference in the world, then four principles follow:

> **► *Power Is About Making a Difference in the World***
>
> PRINCIPLE 1   Power is about altering the states of others.
>
> PRINCIPLE 2   Power is part of every relationship and interaction.
>
> PRINCIPLE 3   Power is found in everyday actions.
>
> PRINCIPLE 4   Power comes from empowering others in social networks.

Let's outline the reasoning underlying these principles. We make a difference in the world by altering others' states (Principle 1). Therefore power is part of every interaction and every relationship (Principle 2). Given these two principles, power is dynamic, in flux, and it is found in everyday acts in our ordinary lives (Principle 3). Accordingly, power is not located within us; it is distributed across social networks and lies in empowering others (Principle 4). Examining the argument and evidence that yields these four principles is the task of this chapter.

POWER IS ABOUT ALTERING THE STATES OF OTHERS

If the social sciences tend to conceptualize power in terms of money, military might, and political participation, it is for good reason: actions within these realms can make a big difference in the world. But if power pervades all social dynamics, then we need to redefine it to illuminate how people make a difference in the world in ways that don't involve money, military action, or politics.

Power, then, is the capacity to alter the state of others. By *state*, I simply mean the condition of another person or other people. States can be about anything—an individual's bank account, a belief, an emotion, physical health, the ability to vote, a feeling of being watched, or a pattern of activation in the brain or response in the immune system.

Defining power in this way better positions us to understand how power has many forms and how we influence others in multifaceted ways. We can influence the economic state of another person by altering her wages, wealth, job security, or retirement savings, or by giving him a gift that lifts him out of privation or by directing capital to her or to the collective that enables her work. We can alter his political state, the access he enjoys to the political process, her likelihood of voting, his sense of political voice, or her feeling of national pride or shame.

We can alter an individual's knowledge about the world. Indeed, profound social change often begins in shifts in understanding the world. In the eighteenth century, three-quarters of the world's people were enslaved, and large portions of European economies were founded upon the slave triangle: shipping goods to Africa, transporting captured slaves to the Caribbean, where those slaves worked the sugarcane fields, then delivering the desired substance to Europeans. What undid this power structure? Knowledge. One day a Cambridge University student, Thomas Clarkson, submitted an essay on the brutalities of the slave trade to a local contest. It won and was passed on to some Quakers, who brought Clarkson into their small network of abolitionists. Energized, Clarkson traveled thousands of miles throughout the United Kingdom interviewing those who had experienced slavery in the Caribbean, reporting his discoveries in essays and pamphlets. His revelations stirred boycotts, aroused the consciences of leaders in the Houses of Lords and Commons, and eventually led to the end of slavery.

We enjoy power in altering the physical states of others. Virginia Apgar was the first female full professor at Columbia University College of Physicians and Surgeons. In 1952, tired of seeing MDs deem premature babies too weak to survive and allowing them to die, she introduced the Apgar score, a ten-point measure of a neonate's breathing, heart rate, complexion, reflexes, and muscular activity, gathered at one and five minutes after birth. Its spread into medical practice has saved hundreds of thousands of lives and raised our awareness of the costs of premature births, which are one out of nine births in the United States today, and which drain $26.2 billion a year out of the U.S. economy. We influence others by changing their physical condition.

Power lies in altering the tastes, preferences, and opinions of others. In creating new food preferences and dietary habits, fast-food pioneers have arguably influenced the collective health of nations as powerfully as all but a few advances in medicine. Vidal Sassoon's "ready-to-wear" haircut from the 1960s shifted women's preferences for what their hair could look like and at the same time freed women from hours of fussing with curlers and sprays, making it just a bit easier to get to work outside the home. Lady Gaga has had a revolutionary influence through her music on how teens understand their sexuality and gender, providing them a language and a public forum to express their ever-evolving identities.

Power, understood as a way of altering the states of others, helps make sense of how influential art, music, satire, and the written word can be. These forms of creative expression may not directly alter a person's bank account or prove decisive on the battlefield, but they are powerful because they alter a person's beliefs about what is real, true, and fair. Dear Abby's writings have helped tens of millions of people navigate the moral dilemmas of everyday life—how to talk to a teenage daughter about depression, what to do about a philandering husband, how to get along with a difficult in-law. Rush Limbaugh, Glenn Beck, Jon Stewart, Stephen Colbert, *The Onion*, and *Saturday Night Live* offer some of the most powerful representations of today's political events. Cultural figures such as Martha Stewart, Bono, LeBron James, Edward Snowden, Arianna Huffington, and Oprah Winfrey are framing and shifting our political leanings, what we deem to be right and good. At its core, power is about altering the states of other people.

POWER IS PART OF EVERY RELATIONSHIP AND INTERACTION

One hundred and seventy years ago, when members of the typical British family sat down to enjoy a cup of tea, they might have done so with the earthenware Victorian-era tea set of the 1840s (see the photo on the next page). It was mass-produced for the middle class, with lacy silver patterns gracing the teapot, the sugar bowl, and the milk jug. As that British family drank their tea, they were participating in the power politics of the British Empire. To fill that unassuming teapot, the British fought two wars with China, the Opium Wars, and grabbed land in India and Ceylon, where they created cheap pools of labor to harvest the leaves of the national drink. To sweeten that drink with sugar, the British elite ran the slave trade. The lesson here is that power imbues every manufactured object: in how it is invented and produced, in how it alters the states of others, in the resources needed to possess it, and in how it signals a specific rank in society.

In social relationships as well, power imbues every interaction and every relationship. Social psychology—my discipline—long assumed that certain categories of relationships were free of power dynamics—for example, those between young lovers or between parent and child. Certainly momentary experiences within these kinds of relationships—the merging with someone as we fall in love, the euphoric delight of wrestling with a dog pile of giggling four-year-olds—suggest that certain relationships are indeed free of rank, influence, and power.

But more recently, intensive studies from around the world have found that power is part of every relationship. Yes, in certain relationships power is more salient and explicit—chiefdoms of a few thousand years ago, military units, religious hierarchies, caste systems in India and other countries, and organizational charts depicting roles within corporations. But upon closer study, all relationships prove to be defined by mutual influence. A developing fetus and its mother are actually competitively vying for nutrients the mother has produced in the womb, a competition that helps explain certain pregnancy-related illnesses. Even this most non-hierarchical of relations—that between mother and developing child—is characterized by patterns of mutual influence. Defining power as altering others' states means that power permeates all relationships, in the family, among friends, and in economic exchanges.

Recognizing that all social relationships are imbued with power can provide us with insight into our personal lives. For example, viewed through this new lens on power, sibling relations may appear in a different light. I feel as though I share as much with my brother, Rolf, as with any other human being alive. We see the world through a similar, genetically encoded, historically shaped lens. But I am older, and that power dynamic influenced how we developed into the individuals we are today.

Early in development, older siblings are bigger, more physically coordinated, and more advanced in language, reasoning, and physical independence. They enjoy greater power over their younger siblings. Many conflicts between very young siblings— upward of six to eight a day—are about power. Out of these power dynamics, siblings develop identities in enduring ways. If you are an older sibling, you are more likely to develop into someone who seeks out power (and study it perhaps), who is a bit more oriented to the status quo (because it has historically favored those like you), and who is a bit more conventional. If you are a younger sibling, you learn to be more sophisticated at the practices of kindness and cooperation, to avoid conflict with your dictatorial older siblings. You are more likely to gravitate toward innovative, risky actions that challenge the status quo, which has been biased against you. You are more likely to endorse and lead scientific revolutions. You are more likely to steal bases as professional baseball players. You are more likely to go into a career as a stand-up comedian and mock the powers that be. We can trace our identities back to the power dynamics of our early family life.

The ebbs and flows of our romantic lives take place within the patterns of power dynamics. The love that partners feel toward each other is colored by the balance of power between them. In more egalitarian, mutually empowered couples, partners feel more

love, more trust, and more satisfaction. But in heterosexual relationships where the woman feels disempowered, she is less likely
to have orgasms and is more likely to lack sexual interest and lu-
brication of her vaginal walls in preparation for sex. In heterosexual couples where the man feels disempowered, for example by
a job loss or an economic downturn, he is more vulnerable to premature ejaculation or erectile dysfunction. Sexual desire cannot be
separated from power, nor can its poetic partner, love.

Theorists have long argued that in friendships we form relations defined by sameness, equality, and reciprocity. And clearly
this is true. At the same time, though, friendships occur within
social networks that are colored by power dynamics. A study of
childhood friendships found that the children with dense networks of friends enjoyed many perks of power—they got more
invitations to birthday parties and playdates, and greater respect
from their peers. Those children who were not named as often as
friends were more likely to suffer the pains of powerlessness—
social rejection, shame, humiliation, and the desire to strike out in
frustration.

The parent-child relationship is imbued with power in innumerable ways, from how a parent handles a four-year-old's temper
tantrums to how a teen follows the parent's decree to not take
drugs. The photo on the next page comes from an eight-mile bike
ride my family took through the psychedelic canyons of Zion National Park. During the ride, I gave my daughters, Natalie and
Serafina, then ten and eight, a handful of M&Ms after each half
mile; good work deserves rewards, after all, the psychologist in me

reasoned. Halfway into the ride, reason got the better of me, and chocolate got the better of them, so I declared that I would dole out no more treats for their efforts. My daughters countered with the emotional display in the photo (taken on the ride). Within milliseconds I was reaching into my pocket to give them more M&Ms.

How people parent emerges out of their stance toward power. Parents who express their authority but empower children with voice and independence produce higher-functioning kids than parents whose styles are anarchic or who are rigidly hierarchical and coercive and who decree from positions of absolute authority what is right and wrong.

Power is not restricted to boardrooms, battlefields, and the U.S. Senate floor. There are plenty of politics on playgrounds, in bedrooms, at dinner tables, at offices, and in bars. Defining power as a capacity to alter the states of others helps clarify how and why it permeates all social interactions, in relationships of every kind.

POWER IS FOUND IN EVERYDAY ACTIONS

Social psychologists have long used "the leaderless group discussion paradigm" to study who rises in power. A group of strangers is brought together and asked to solve a problem collectively, like choosing from among different candidates for a job, dividing a pool of money, or even rank ordering objects, such as a flashlight, mirror, knife, and canteen, in terms of which would be most useful for surviving alone in a desert for a week. Roles are not assigned, and no guidance is provided; the individuals are left to their own devices to discuss and reach consensus on a decision, all the while being videotaped.

While making the decision, some of the participants gain power—very quickly. Outside observers viewing the videotapes of these interactions will agree within a minute or so about who has power and who does not. People quickly fold into patterns of influence that others can perceive. Power emerges instantaneously when humans interact. The same is true in children's interactions. When ten-to-twelve-year-old boys settle into summer camp life, within a day some campers enjoy more power and are shaping their group dynamics. When children go to kindergarten, shortly after the start of school some five-year-olds are perceived by their peers to have more influence, and others less so. Even among children as young as two, some quickly enjoy more influence at day care, in that they attract attention, guide play, and control valuable resources—the cherished scooter or the favorite tire swing.

Power is always emerging, quickly, as the leaderless group discussion paradigm reveals. People gain power as the result of small, everyday behaviors: by speaking up first, offering a possible answer to a problem, being first to assert an opinion, freeing up everyone's thinking by throwing out a wild suggestion, question, or humorous observation that gets the creative juices flowing.

Our power is found in simple acts that bind people together and yield the greatest benefits for the group. The difference we make in the world depends on the quotidian: on raising the right question, offering encouragement, connecting people who don't know one another, suggesting a new idea. Power is surprisingly available in daily acts of social life. Critical to avoiding the power paradox is recognizing that enduring power hinges on doing simple things that are good for others.

The fact that power is tied to everyday acts helps explain why it is always in flux. Your capacity to influence is always shifting, depending on your actions. A person's power differs from one context to another: a woman might feel powerful supervising a team at work but relatively powerless at home when negotiating with a defiant teen. Even within the same context, a person's power shifts over time: one day at work the individual is assertive and influential, the next day less so.

Studies of our primate relatives and hunter-gatherers also provide evidence for this third principle, that power is context specific, continually shifting, and dependent upon specific actions tailored to the current situation. Despotic species like gorillas and chimpanzees routinely resort to threat and coercion to rule, but their rank—that is, their influence and access to resources—is negotiated nearly every hour of every day between alpha males and females and their rivals. Even in more hierarchical species, rank may be in flux and tied to context. Anthropologists who studied hunter-gatherers in New Guinea, Alaska, the Amazon, and Africa found it difficult, if not impossible, to identify a single leader. Instead, the individuals who had power shifted from one context to another, and it was tied to specific actions relevant to the needs of the group. An individual's capacity for influence—power—is found in ordinary actions tailored to specific contexts that advance the group's interests.

POWER COMES FROM EMPOWERING OTHERS
IN SOCIAL NETWORKS

Charles Darwin changed the world with *On the Origin of Species*, but much of his evidence came from the network he created. He carefully wrote fifteen hundred letters a year, or about four a day, to collaborators who included missionaries in remote parts of the world, a French neurologist working on facial musculature, MDs reporting on when patients blush, fur trappers, gardeners, zookeepers, and pigeon fanciers. Darwin's writings are an expression of many people's ideas from all walks of life.

What appears to be an influential act of an individual typically will prove to be a collaboration of many minds, the action of a social network. Work today is more collaborative than ever, founded upon the networking tendencies Darwin so excelled at more than a century and a half ago. Half the U.S. workforce is working in teams. A study of over 19 million scientific papers from the past fifty years found that the number of authors on those papers has nearly doubled over that time. The same is true of patents. Acts of innovation and influence are collaborative. We have arrived at our fourth principle: power is distributed across social networks and is found in empowering others.

No one got this more right than the philosopher Hannah Arendt. While living in Berlin in the early 1930s, Arendt was active in fighting the rise of Nazism. She was apprehended, interrogated, and released by the SS and shortly thereafter left Germany. An early critic of Stalinism and a champion of equal status for Israelis and Palestinians, she found lasting renown in an essay for *The New Yorker* in which she argued that Nazi mastermind Adolf Eichmann was not the sadistic psychopath whom all had imagined, prior to his trial in Jerusalem, but just a functionary signing papers within Hitler's bureaucracy. The power of the Nazi state did not reside within evil individuals but was distributed across the networks of that power-mad social system.

In *The Origins of Totalitarianism*, Arendt detailed distinctions between slavery, totalitarian states, and the Holocaust and explained how such oppressive hierarchies, founded upon coercive force, strip individuals of their power, their ability to make a difference in the world. Guiding these observations is her conceptualization of power:

> *Power corresponds to the human ability not just to act but to act in concert. Power is never the property of an individual; it belongs to a group and remains in existence only so long as the group keeps together. When we say of somebody that he is "in power," we actually refer to his being empowered by a certain number of people to act in their name.*

Elsewhere Arendt writes that power is the ability to "stir others to collective action." The French philosopher Michel Foucault would agree, proposing that power is "employed and exercised through a net-like organization." Your capacity to influence others depends upon the networks of people you are connected to, which today means your 300 Facebook friends, the 1,200 people you know, your family and circle of six to eight friends (all averages in the United States), and the extent to which those individuals influence others, who in turn influence others, who in turn influence others, and so on.

Arendt's thesis—that power is found in one's capacity to stir others within social networks—has deep evolutionary roots. We evolved in small groups of a few dozen individuals. We lived in centralized camps, where we cooked, ate, played, fought, reproduced, and slept in close contact and typically collaboratively, moving around as necessary to accommodate others, and taking care of children. Our digestive systems, adapted to protein-dense meat, coevolved with the cooperative hunting of big game, which is rare in the primate world. We fought and defended ourselves collectively against other hominids who had branched off from our evolutionary tree. We built up collaborative networks to take care of our big-brained, hypervulnerable offspring. That is, in evolution we met critical survival- and reproduction-related problems by collaborating in social networks. Our power as a species was social and was found in the actions of social collectives. Today as well, an individual has power to the extent that she stirs those social collectives to take purposeful, effective action.

If our power is found in our social networks, then it follows that it is based in how well we empower others. And we empower others through daily acts of influence: by acknowledging another's good work, by offering an encouraging phrase or making appreciative eye contact, or by giving others responsibilities, resources, and opportunities. That power lies in empowering individuals in social networks is in fact an antidote to the power paradox. Desmond Tutu concurs. When asked how he helped bring down apartheid in South Africa, he replied: It was the result of small actions of millions of individuals.

Our everyday actions within social networks can be catalysts of influence and social change. If you change your diet to consume less meat, your neighbors are likely to do the same. If you give to charities, your work colleagues laboring nearby are more likely to do so as well. If you vote and talk about it with your friends, they are more likely to vote. Behavior is infectious. When you share something with a stranger, that act of generosity makes the stranger 19 percent more generous in a subsequent interaction with new strangers not involving you. That new stranger, in turn, is 7 percent more generous in yet another interaction with yet other strangers, now twice removed from you. If you do things that boost your happiness, it will not only boost your friend's happiness, it will also lift the spirits of your friend's friend, someone you don't even know. Power is found in empowering others in our social networks.

THE POWER PARADOX BEGINS

In this chapter we have uncovered four principles that illuminate what power is. It is the capacity to alter others' states. It permeates interactions in all social relationships. It is continually emerging and in flux according to everyday actions. It is distributed across social networks and is found in empowering others.

Having power—a capacity for influence—feels good, in a particular way. It does not feel soothing or calm or blissed out.

Rather, it is accompanied by feelings of enthusiasm, inspiration, and hope, and it is supported by surges of dopamine in the brain. This feeling of power leads us to seek power and to enjoy it when we are making a difference in the world. But beware of enjoying the lofty delights of power too much: dopamine and the feelings of power are at the heart of addictions to certain drugs, like cocaine, and bouts of mania, both of which lead to impulsive, unethical action and delusional thought. What feels so good—the capacity to influence and make a difference in the world—can quickly turn to excess. The power paradox is always close by.

2.

Power Is Given,
Not Grabbed

first read *Lord of the Flies* when I was fifteen, and my family was on sabbatical in Nottingham, England—for me, the misty land of Robin Hood and D. H. Lawrence. William Golding's tale of the shipwrecked boys' descent into depravity—with painted faces, chants, torture of Piggy, and thirst for blood—seemed to resemble the recession-mired England I came to know that year: a place of bullying, teachers humiliating hooligans, fifteen-year-olds getting drunk at pubs, and skirmishes between the punks and the Teddy boys at school dances.

At the heart of *Lord of the Flies* is a thought experiment known as the "natural state experiment," first described by the philosopher Thomas Aquinas some eight hundred years ago. This experiment asks, What are people like if you put them in a context in which civilization is stripped away, leaving them to behave in their natural state? Absent, in Golding's terms, "the protection of parents and school and policemen and the law," what do people do? For many, answers to such thought experiments reveal Machiavellian assumptions about human nature: that free of the structures and strictures of society, our base and violent tendencies spring forth.

Lord of the Flies begins with an election. The boys are to choose between Ralph, who is respectful, calm, and physically imposing, and Jack, who is obsessed with weaponry, meat, tribal markings, and killing the island's pigs. The boys cast their first votes for Ralph and start forming a society with democratic dialogue, rules, schedules, and duties. It is only a matter of time, though, before Jack grabs power. He converts the young boys to his cause with face painting. He rules his recruits through coercive bouts of bullying and by telling them chilling tales of supernatural monsters hovering in the forest nearby. By the end of the book, Jack and his tribe are hunting down Ralph as their cannibalistic calls pierce the air.

Natural state thought experiments are a mainstay in debates about human nature. Remove the moral codes and conventions of society, and what instincts guide human behavior? What laws are most essential? What principles should guide the allocation of resources? And who gains power as groups form? On this last question, many believe that it is the more coercive, forceful, and violent individuals who earn the respect of their peers and gain power. But this belief will not fare well in the science we are about to tour.

For the past twenty years I have been carrying out natural state experiments to find out how power is distributed in groups.

I have infiltrated college dorms and children's summer camps to document who rises in power. I have brought entire sororities and fraternities into the lab, capturing the substance and spread of individuals' reputations within their social networks. I have surreptitiously identified which members of groups are gossiped about, and who receives gossip. The findings from this research converge on the organizing idea of this chapter. Whereas the Machiavellian approach to power assumes that individuals grab it through coercive force, strategic deception, and the undermining of others, the science finds that power is not grabbed but is given to individuals by groups.

What this means is that your ability to make a difference in the world is shaped by what other people think of you. Your capacity to alter the state of others depends on their trust in you. Your ability to empower others depends on their willingness to be influenced by you. Your power is constructed in the judgments and actions of others. This idea distills down to four principles:

Numerous natural state experiments demonstrate that Jack's strategies of bullying, coercion, and violence do not prevail; rather, groups demonstrate an instinctive tendency to give power to individuals who bring the greatest benefit and least harm to individuals, to those who advance the greater good (Principle 5). To make abuses of power less likely, groups shape people's capacity to influence by constructing their reputations, which track their contributions to the greater good (Principle 6). Groups reward those who are good for the group by affording them elevated status and esteem (Principle 7). And when an individual acts in ways that violate the greater good—the group's sense of its collective

> ### Power Is Given, Not Grabbed

PRINCIPLE 5   Groups give power to those who advance the
greater good.

PRINCIPLE 6   Groups construct reputations that determine the
capacity to influence.

PRINCIPLE 7   Groups reward those who advance the greater good
with status and esteem.

PRINCIPLE 8   Groups punish those who undermine the greater good
with gossip.

welfare—the group will resort to gossip and other reputational damage to diminish the influence of that individual (Principle 8).

These four principles center on a concept known as the greater good. This idea emerged from the eighteenth-century philosophical movement known as utilitarianism, in which philosophers Francis Hutcheson, Jeremy Bentham, and later John Stuart Mill used measurement and quantification to define what makes an action a good one to take. Their answer: an action is good to the degree that it advances the greater good, or what we might today call the collective well-being of a social network or, more broadly, the trust or strength of a society. Or as Hutcheson put it, "That action is best, which procures the greatest happiness for the greatest numbers, and that worst which, in like manner, occasions misery."

Any action that an individual engages in, or more generally a person's character, can be given a "greater good score": the degree to which it benefits others and does not bring harm. Of course, there are complexities in assigning greater good scores to actions and to people's character. Such judgments involve making inferences about their intentions, and humans routinely engage in actions with good intentions but that harm many, like a misguided financial adviser who bets his clients' wealth on an investment that he believes will be a good one, but proves to be wrong. And judging the harms and benefits of an action must take into consideration the unfolding of its consequences over time, in both the short and the long term. For example, Thomas Clarkson's publicizing of the atrocities of slavery in the United Kingdom initially upset some but in the long run inspired actions that enhanced the well-being of many.

Granting these complexities, people do have a fairly keen sense in judging whether actions are good or bad for many. Those who earn high greater good scores are those who advance the interests of many and produce little harm, like an individual who performs an act of charity or Clarkson's inspiring the ending of UK slavery, an elderly woman who starts a local recycling campaign, a child who consoles another who's been bullied, or a manager who directs resources in ways that greatly enhance an organization's reach and bottom line. Conversely, actions that harm many and benefit few would earn low greater good scores, like an act of hate speech, planting a humiliating video on the Internet, a school shooting, or knowingly creating a financial product that will reduce the savings of many.

When individuals act in ways that yield high greater good

scores, their groups fare better. Such actions produce greater trust among group members, enable robust cooperation, make for more proficient action, and give groups a competitive edge. As for people with power, to the extent that they act in ways that benefit the greater good, those they influence should prosper, be they small groups (friends at school, units and committees at work, teams, and neighborhoods) or larger ones (ideological parties, activist groups, online communities, states, and nations). Groups of all kinds fare better when individuals act in ways that promote the greater good.

What is more surprising is how pivotal promoting the greater good is to the distribution of power within social groups. In fact, it is the central consideration in the minds of social collectives in giving power to individuals. Groups are collectively wary of coercive, Machiavellian types, like Jack in *Lord of the Flies*, for the simple reason that if they are left unchecked, they will undermine the smooth functioning of the group. Groups are savvy to abuses of power, aware that once people are in power, they can quickly devolve into self-serving gratification machines, feeling entitled, at times, to harm others for their own gain. Many social practices that we will consider in this chapter are finely attuned to those who undermine the greater good.

During the Age of Enlightenment, utilitarian philosophers developed the idea of the greater good to understand happiness and the good life. But humans have been concerned about the greater good for much longer, and this notion guides the dynamics of the distribution of power.

GROUPS GIVE POWER TO THOSE WHO ADVANCE THE GREATER GOOD

Natural state thought experiments, like *Lord of the Flies*, are theoretically compelling but are difficult to pull off scientifically. As we enter just about any situation—arriving at kindergarten for the first day, socializing in college, joining the workforce, or making friends on Facebook—we already belong to a social class, a neighborhood, a family with a lineage and history, and an ethnic tribe. But a dorm hall at a large public university is a good choice for such an experiment. The late teen years are a developmental period when young women and men become acutely aware of their power; their social rank says a great deal about the social gatherings they will be invited to and what kind of sexual life they will enjoy or be reduced to yearning for. The standardized conditions of dorm life—nine-by-twelve-foot rooms, a shared address, and mass-produced cafeteria food—minimize class-related differences of neighborhood, lifestyle, and domicile.

Mindful of these concerns, some twenty years ago I secured the participation of one hall in a first-year dorm at the University of Wisconsin in Madison. Some of the students were wealthy, some were middle class, and some were poor, which is to say that they were representative of the distribution of wealth and class in the United States. My plan was to carry out a natural state experiment and document who rose to power.

At the start of the semester, I visited the dorm and had students indicate how much "influence" every other person on their hall had. They also filled out a questionnaire that asked them to report on the extent to which their own personalities are defined by five social tendencies, five general ways of acting in the world, known as the Big Five. In the table below I've listed the Big Five in colloquial terms—as enthusiasm, kindness, focus, calmness, and openness—along with related actions that undermine or advance the greater good.

The Big Five: Five Social Tendencies and Their Contribution to the Greater Good

Social Tendency—Actions with High Greater Good Score	Actions with Low Greater Good Score
Enthusiasm—Reach out to others	Avoid social contact
Kindness—Cooperate, share, give	Exploit others for own gain
Focus—Focus on shared goals, rules	Neglect shared goals, rules
Calmness—Instill calm, perspective	Complain, be defensive
Openness—Be open to others' ideas and feelings	Disregard others' ideas

I returned four months later, and then again at the nine-month point, to ask participants to again report on their fellow dorm members' power. For each person in the dorm, I tallied up all the other dorm members' ratings of his or her power at the start, middle, and end of the academic year. I found that power flowed quickly to certain individuals: by two weeks into the school year, some students already had more power than others. And I found flux: every student's level of power in his or her peers' eyes fluctu-ated over the year.

Who rose to power? Who did the groups give power to (Prin-ciple 5) and construct more favorable reputations of (Principles 6 and 7)? We have a deep cultural intuition that nice guys finish last, that one must step on others to rise in the ranks, and that acquiring power requires the cold-blooded dispensing of rivals and even allies. But nothing could have been further from the truth. In my experiment, the strongest predictor of which dorm dwellers rose to the top within the first week of arriving at col-lege, and which ones remained there through the year, was en-thusiasm. The other Big Five mattered as well: kindness, focus, calmness, and openness also related to students' power.

I went on to replicate these findings in a Vanderbilt sorority, in a Wisconsin fraternity, in Berkeley dorms, and even in a sum-mer basketball camp. But studies that rely solely on U.S. college students are limited in profound ways. Young adults, typically from middle- or upper-class backgrounds, enjoying the freedom of college and the privileges of an advanced education, are a thin slice of humanity, and data coming from them may not say much about the world outside the ivory tower.

Other social psychologists have studied who rises in power in different arenas. In financial firms, hospitals, and manufacturing plants, they track who is promoted to high-level management po-sitions or is judged to be effective as a leader. In schools, they track those who serve on student council, those whom their peers regard as good leaders, and those who are popular (Principles 6 and 7). In the military, they track which recruits become officers. The samples are diverse with respect to social class, gender, and ethnicity. And across all seventy studies, those who rose to power were those who had all of the Big Five.

Groups give us power when we are *enthusiastic*, speak up, make bold assertions, and express an interest in others. Our capacity to influence rises when we practice *kindness*, express appreciation, cooperate, and dignify what others say and do. We are more likely to make a difference in the world when we are *focused*, articulate clear purposes and courses of action, and keep others on task. We rise in power when we provide *calm* and remind people of broader perspectives during times of stress, tell stories that calm during times of tension, and practice kind speech. Our opportunity for influence increases when we are *open* and ask great questions, listen to others with receptive minds, and offer playful ideas and novel perspectives. The Big Five concept captures different ways in which we, in the words of Hannah Arendt, "stir others to collective action" and advance the greater good.

In hunter-gatherer societies as well, groups give power to those who advance the greater good. A definitive summary of forty-eight studies found that those who rise to power are "generous (i.e., kind), brave in combat, wise in making subsistence or military decisions, apt at resolving intragroup conflicts, a good speaker, fair, impartial (i.e., open), reliable (focused), tactful (calm), and morally upright," and "strong and assertive" (enthusiastic) but "humble." As one might expect, hunter-gatherer groups give power to those who are courageous and can handle conflict well, but the greater-good-enhancing characteristics of the Big Five are just as pivotal. There is no evidence that Jack's coercive violence is a path to power in hunter-gatherer societies.

Principle 5—groups give power to individuals who advance the greater good—may even be at work among our primate relatives, the chimpanzees. Just after completing his PhD, the primatologist Frans de Waal spent six months observing a community of chimps at the Royal Burgers' Zoo in Arnhem, Netherlands, eventually distilling his observations into his book *Chimpanzee Politics.*

At the outset of de Waal's study, one male chimp, Yeroen, ruled over the community, enjoying the best food, extended periods of being groomed, and unfettered access to sexually active females. Then Luit, a large, younger male, mounted a challenge to Yeroen and after six months replaced him as the alpha male. Importantly, Luit did not resort to coercion or violence to gain power—in more than one thousand observed encounters between Yeroen and Luit, they came to blows only five times. Instead, as with humans, it was Luit's ability to enhance the welfare of the other chimps that paved his way to power. He groomed and embraced the other chimps—contributing social resources to others (Principle 5). He demonstrated an ability to keep the peace within the community (Principle 6). He was rewarded with deferential bows and submissive smiles, signs of chimpanzee esteem (Principle 7). In de Waal's words: "A leader receives support and respect from the group . . . in exchange for keeping order."

In primate social life, human and nonhuman alike, groups give power to those who advance the greater good. This basic power

Frans de Waal observing some
chimpanzees at the Royal Burgers' Zoo in Arnhem, Netherlands

Nikkie greeting Yeroen in submissive fashion. Ritualized submissive displays involve crouching posture, grunts, and grimaces, and convey status to higher-power chimps, and are precursors to how we express our esteem of high-status individuals.

Yeroen chasing Luit. It is interesting to note that in this photo, with his power slipping, Yeroen resorts to more severe threat displays.

dynamic ensures that groups are led by individuals who will not be their undoing but will instead act with enthusiasm, kindness, focus, calm, and openness, thereby benefiting the groups.

GROUPS CONSTRUCT REPUTATIONS THAT DETERMINE THE CAPACITY TO INFLUENCE

The most famous letter in American literature would have to be the *A* in Nathaniel Hawthorne's *The Scarlet Letter.* Who could forget the *A* sewn onto Hester Prynne's seventeenth-century blouse, the reminder of her affair with a charismatic young minister, Arthur Dimmesdale, which at the time was a reprehensible act and the basis for social ostracism? The luminous *A* burns on Hester's chest and in her mind like a blush of shame. As she makes her rounds through Salem, Massachusetts, eyes fasten upon the *A*; it triggers whispers, sniggers, and scurrilous speculations from the town gossips. It isolates her daughter, Pearl, offspring of her sin, who suffers the cruel mockery of other children in town.

The Scarlet Letter is a timeless meditation upon a universal social obsession, reputation, which is the focus of our next power principle, Principle 6: a person's capacity to influence is shaped by his or her reputation within a group. Reputation is the judgment of an individual's character arrived at by a social collective. At its core, reputation is about character, trust, and integrity, or the capacity to advance the greater good.

Hester Prynne's *A* defines her reputation, largely sexual in substance. But what does the *A* stand for today, in this era of greater sexual freedom and self-expression? To answer this question, I recruited a dorm at the University of California, Berkeley. In the fall and again in the spring, students came to the lab individually and in an open-ended, conversational way talked about their impressions of the character of two randomly selected students in their dorm. Only rarely did the participants refer to the two students' self-expression or sexual purity. Instead, they were concerned with whether the individual treated others in kind, respectful, cooperative ways—in actions promoting the greater good. After only one week of living together, participants already spoke of some students who were cold, selfish, deceptive, and inconsiderate. They were marking them with reputations that would shape their influence in the dorm (Principle 6).

What's true of reputations in college dorms is true at work as well. Everyone in a workplace knows who the bad apples are— those who have reputations for undermining the organization's cohesiveness. Bad apples are rude and uncivil, they free-ride on others' efforts, and they complain and quarrel and instigate uncivil discourse. These reputations cost them—they tend to not rise in power, and they enjoy few opportunities for influence or innovation (Principle 6).

Historically, punishment of those whose actions undermined the greater good was more primitive. In seventeenth-century Germany, when village dwellers acted in ways that undermined the sense of community, they were required to wear shame masks, or *Schandmasken*, that matched their uncivil acts. For example, people behaving boorishly wore pig masks with giant snouts, as penance for drunken behavior, grotesque eating, or greed (all minor abuses of power that we shall consider in Chapter 4). As individuals made their way through town wearing their shame masks, they were ridiculed and mocked, suffering stinging losses in social status (Principles 7 and 8).

People arrive quickly at intuitions about whether others are community minded and are likely to advance the greater good. These intuitions feed into the casual conversations that define group life and determine individuals' reputations. For example, in investment banking and financial analysis firms, individuals quickly gain reputations as collaborative colleagues or as people out for their own gain, and when those individuals move to a new project, the new team members already know of their reputations, even though they may never have actually met. Such reputations persist over time, from one year to the next, remaining in the minds of their colleagues, guiding daily interactions.

By constructing reputations, groups shape an individual's capacity for influence—Principle 6—in two distinct ways. First, reputations create opportunities for influence. Studies find that if you have a reputation for advancing the greater good, others will direct more resources to you. They will seek you out to form friendships and alliances. They will collaborate with you more cooperatively and effectively. People with reputations for being selfish and out for personal gain, by contrast, tend to be excluded from exciting areas of innovation and collaboration and occupy more peripheral places within social networks. Reputations are amplifiers of the capacity to influence.

Second, reputations are a group's way of making individuals aware of the effects of their actions upon others, increasing the

A shame mask.

chances they will in the future act in ways that are good for the group. To get a sense of this, look for a moment at the geometric shape above.

Did it trigger any feelings? Any sensations in your body— maybe a slight heating of your cheeks? This pattern of dots captures the geometric arrangement of the eyes and mouth on the human face. Seeing it evokes the sense that someone is looking at you, watching you, and ready to form opinions about your reputation. Researchers find that even incidental exposure to this abstract image makes people more generous to others.

In that study, participants were given a sum of money and asked to write down on a sheet of paper the amount, including none at all, that they would give to a stranger. Off to the side on the answer sheet, they saw either the pattern of three dots minimally evocative of the human face, or the same dots configured upside down. Simply seeing the dots evocative of the face reduced by half the participants' selfish tendency to give no money to a stranger. An awareness of reputation brings out our better tendencies.

Groups actively construct reputations of those who form them, focusing on a person's capacity to advance the greater good. Reputations create opportunities for influence and the awareness of being judged by others, reminding the influential that their power is fleeting and rests in the judgments of others. Reputations prompt the powerful to act in cooperative, altruistic ways. When the powerful lose their focus on what others think of them—a myopia that readily accompanies power—they all too quickly act in impulsive ways that undermine the greater good, thus losing power. Reputation is one way groups attempt to prevent the power paradox. Another way is the awarding of esteem.

GROUPS REWARD THOSE WHO ADVANCE THE GREATER GOOD WITH STATUS AND ESTEEM

Over the course of our evolution, food sharing has been a central means by which humans build social networks and direct esteem to those who give to the group (Principle 7). Among the Netsilik Inuit, each individual is assigned twelve food-sharing partners whom they keep throughout their lives. Anytime an individual within one of these networks kills a seal, that person carefully cuts it up into fourteen parts and shares twelve pieces with his or her partners, keeping two for him- or herself. The sharing of food solidifies and maintains social ties.

In preindustrial cultures like the Netsilik, groups elevate the status of individuals in proportion to the amount of food they share. In the highlands of New Guinea, neighboring tribes gather every year in celebration to ritualistically give away food they have cultivated—piles of yams, pig carcasses, and arrays of coconuts. The more an individual gives away, the higher the status he or she will enjoy. This same dynamic accounts for the laws of meat sharing in sub-Saharan Africa, in the Inuit tribes of the Arctic, and among the dwellers of the Amazon. Generous food sharers whose acts of largesse burnish their reputations fare better in evolutionary terms: more generous men have greater access to mates and produce more offspring; more generous women enjoy greater care for their children from others.

These offerings of seal meat, yams, and meat traded for the respect of one's peers speak to a more general principle related to the distribution of power: groups give status to individuals in exchange for actions that advance the greater good (Principle 7). Status is the esteem an individual enjoys in the judgments of others; it is the positivity of an individual's reputation. Very often power and status go together. For example, we esteem individuals in careers that have a large capacity to influence—medical doctors, judges, and teachers. People making a difference in the world enjoy the esteem of those around them and elevated status in society.

But status and power are separable. It is possible to have power without status. The corrupt politician or Wall Street financier is held in low esteem by many but influences others in profound ways through political action or the flow of capital. Conversely, people can enjoy elevated status without much power. Professors

often fit the bill, with honorific titles next to their names and respect in society, but many toil away on obscure ideas that often
have little influence in the world. These distinctions tell us that
social collectives can rely on a precious social resource—status—
to shape the behavior of individuals with power.

Group members reward individuals who advance the greater
good by affording them status in a rich language of behaviors
that evolved out of primate deference displays. (For an example,
see the photo on page 53 of a chimpanzee named Nikkie greeting
the more powerful Yeroen and think back to times when you cow-
ered and stammered around someone you respect.) When we
blush, bow, nod our heads, or avert our gaze, we elevate the status
of those we direct these behaviors to, and those individuals feel
valued, empowered, and esteemed. We elevate the status of others
with compliments, flattery, ingratiating comments, public roasts,
awards, and outright praise and adoration. People around the
world systematically use the tactics of politeness—hesitations,
indirectness, apologies, formalities—when speaking with higher-
status individuals. These subtle shifts in phrasing, syntax, and
delivery convey the respect that the speaker feels toward the
recipient.

Being a recipient of these status-affording acts triggers powerful reactions in the brain, updating William James's 130-year-
old assertion that "the deepest principle in human nature is the
craving to be appreciated." In one illustrative study, participants
lying in an fMRI scanner listened to phrases written by their
friends that expressed esteem for them: "You have always stood up

for me when I really needed it." "You give me strength." "You have inspired me to keep going during times of doubt." Hearing these status-elevating expressions activated the dopamine-rich circuits in the participants' ventral striatum, the region of the brain activated by the experience of delight upon eating chocolate or getting a great massage. That is, being esteemed by fellow group members triggers the brain reactions associated with cravings.

When social collectives elevate the status of individuals in formal acts of recognition—such as awards—it inspires others to act in ways that advance the group's interests. When scholarly societies give out prestigious awards that recognize an individual's contributions, productivity in the area of the individual's interest increases; the pursuit of status inspires concentrated work and innovation.

Status, then, is precious; it is something that individuals crave and that groups award selectively to inspire magnanimity and hard work. This hunger for elevated status serves groups well, leading to arms races of generosity as individuals compete for status. Examples of such competitive altruism abound in our everyday lives: outrageous bids at a fund-raising auction, gifts to alma maters for named buildings, or young men dirtying their hands and shirts to help an elderly man whose car has broken down.

The affordance of status is yet another means by which groups keep the powerful in check, attempting to countervail the more selfish tendencies that accompany the abuses of power. Should those with power no longer value the high regard of those below them, or misinterpret or make too much of how they are esteemed, they will be subject to a much-maligned social behavior, gossip—

a final means by which groups give power to those who advance the greater good.

GROUPS PUNISH THOSE WHO UNDERMINE THE GREATER GOOD WITH GOSSIP

For many, gossiping ranks among the great sins. Saint Paul placed whispering and backbiting on a par with murder, deceit, and fornication as vices deserving of capital punishment. Teachers routinely ask middle-schoolers to not gossip or whisper with their friends. For good reason: gossip can humiliate and harm in ways that might even shorten lives. Andrew Jackson's wife, Rachel, had left her first marriage to run off with the future president in 1793, when divorce rates hovered between 0 and 5 percent. As a result, she was the target of vicious gossip during Jackson's presidential campaign. When she first read of her damaged reputation, she collapsed in tears. Several weeks later she was dead.

No wonder we bristle at being called a gossip. But these exceptional uses of gossip—typically by those who are abusing their power—do not prove the rule. In fact, gossip is an ancient and universal means by which group members give power to select individuals and keep the powerful in check (Principle 8).

Gossip is how we articulate a person's capacity for advancing the greater good and spread that information to others. We gossip about what might be true of a person's character. When we talk with others about firmly known facts—a neighbor is in prison, a work colleague is a heroin addict in rehab, a friend on the softball team has cancer—we are passing on established information that does not buzz with the energized feel of speculation so true of gossip. We resort to gossip to explore potential flaws in a person's character. Gossip seeks confirmation of character flaws defined by the flouting of principles that enhance the greater good.

Gossip, then, is how a social network negotiates and establishes a person's reputation, in particular those who seek power and want to exert influence in Machiavellian fashion. For example, U.S. presidential campaigns are defined by pitched battles over gossip, which hovers around every candidate and eventually targets every president at some point. Political gossip zeroes in on whether a politician does things that risk unraveling the culture, that are the foundation of the greater good. During the era of slavery, political gossip focused on candidates' racial background. During Prohibition, gossip investigated politicians' alcoholic tendencies and the potential hypocrisies of their imbibing. During the drug wars, the drug-taking habits of politicians became prominent. That gossips today would want to see President Barack Obama's birth certificate should not be surprising in light of our present concern with immigration. Thomas Jefferson had a keen sense for the power of gossip in establishing political reputations. He catalogued the forms of political gossip during his day and concluded that the most damaging centered on selfish, backstabbing, socially destructive acts.

To capture Jefferson's reasoning as it applies to a twenty-first-century social group, I studied the patterns of gossip in a network of sorority sisters at UC Berkeley. In the first phase, I gathered measures of the sisters' Big Five—their enthusiasm, kindness, focus, calm, and openness—and their Machiavellianism, or tendency to lie, manipulate, and coerce. Then several weeks later I brought each sister to the lab and interviewed her privately about how often she gossiped about each of the other women in the sorority, and with whom she shared the gossip. The frequent targets of gossip were young women who most threatened the sorority's greater good: they were well known and highly visible but, by their own reporting, unkind and highly Machiavellian, willing to harm, lie, and manipulate to rise in power. Gossip typically targets individuals who seek power at the expense of others.

Gossip tarnishes the reputations of individuals who diminish the greater good. Researchers who hung around a crew of strapping rowers at an East Coast college listened in on the teammates' banter as they traveled to and from practice. The gossip systematically concentrated on one teammate who was not making practices on time, nor rowing hard enough or in sync with his teammates. He was failing to advance the greater good by literally not pulling his weight. Cattle ranchers in the western United States, in their spare, tight-lipped exchanges, gossiped about their neighbors who didn't keep their fences in order. Again, gossip targets actions that undermine the trust of the community—for ranchers, the poor upkeep of fences. In hunter-gatherer societies, gossip is directed at coercive bullies who exploit others and steal food or sexual partners.

How gossip flows through social networks enhances its power to tarnish the reputations of those who do less to promote the greater good. On average, we pass along every act of gossip we receive to 2.3 people, typically to high-status, highly connected people like, in the sorority study, high-status and admired young women. Gossip flows to individuals who have the greatest power to define, and damage, the reputations of others.

So powerful is the social instinct to gossip that it gave rise to institutions that preserve its basic function. The first newspapers in seventeenth-century England to be widely read and financially sustainable were gossip rags about the neighborhood knaves and ne'er-do-wells, the flirts and drunks, the philanderers and squanderers, and the debauching aristocracy. One of America's wisest citizens, Ben Franklin, wrote a gossip column, the first in America, that appeared in 1814 and was devoted to satirical commentary upon the scurrilous acts of people nearby.

In today's digital world, gossip and the construction of reputations have gone viral on websites and blogs. Restaurants, stores, and hotels anxiously keep an eye on their customer ratings on *Yelp*. Politicians are tracked on *Gawker* and spoofed on *The Onion*. The Shittytipper Twitter feed names well-known individuals known to tip below the conventional 15 to 20 percent. A now defunct blog called *Holla Back NYC* allowed women to submit photos of men who harassed, groped, catcalled, or leered at them.

Our obsession with spreading information about reputation has costs: intrusions into our private lives, mistakes in identity, and escalations into bullying, all indirect forms of oppression. Most of us have been the inappropriate targets of gossip and suffered in the moment. But on balance, the benefits of allowing groups to freely communicate about the reputations of others outweigh these costs.

In one study to first capture this idea, twenty-four participants came to the lab and were divided into groups of four. They played six rounds of an economic game; in every new round they played with participants they had not played with before. In each round, each participant was given some money and presented with the chance to give some money to a group fund. That gift would increase in value and be redistributed among the four players. This game pitted the tendency to act on behalf of others—give money to the group fund—against the free-riding tendency to not contribute yet take money from the group fund built up by others' generosity. At the end of the first round, players learned how much the three other group members had given to the group fund. Participants moved on to a new group of four players and played again, repeating this procedure six times.

After the first round, the study got interesting. In a gossip condition, participants could send a note to those who would be playing with their former partners about those individuals' cooperative or selfish tendencies. As in real life, all players were aware of the possibility that they would be gossiped about. In an even more puritanical condition—gossip plus ostracism—participants had the chance not only to gossip but also to vote to exclude their former partners from playing in the next round.

In a neutral condition lacking the opportunity to gossip or ostracize, people gave less and less to the public fund over time. After trusting others initially but being taken advantage of by the occasional individual with low commitment to the greater good, most people abandon their cooperative instincts and give less. In the condition in which participants could gossip, participants actually gave more. And in the condition allowing for gossip and ostracism, participants' gifts to the group fund actually rose over the course of the experiment.

Social penalties like gossip, shaming, and ostracism are painful indeed and can easily be misused (in particular by those in power). But they are also powerful social practices, seen in all cultures, by which group members elevate the standing of those who advance the greater good and prevent those less committed to it from gaining power.

THE GIFT OF POWER

Exploitative, selfish, coercive behavior unravels the fabric of strong groups. Groups know this and also have histories with individuals who abuse power and act in greedy and impulsive ways. So groups choose to give power to people who are enthusiastic, kind, focused, calm, and open. They construct reputations that track an individual's capacity to act on behalf of the group, and they rely on these reputations to collaborate, cooperate, and build alliances and strong ties. They elevate the status of those who share, and they tarnish the reputations of the selfish and the Machiavellian through delectable acts of gossip. Power is not grabbed. It is given.

3.

Enduring Power Comes from a Focus on Others

The belief that a sacred, living force propels us to make a difference in the world is universal to humanity. And throughout history, making a difference in the world has been seen as one of the most crucial and meaningful aspects of human life. Preindustrial communities expressed this force most vividly in acts of sharing, expertise, and courage and recognized it in clothing, names, and tattoos, often given in sacred rites of passage. The Polynesians called this sacred force *mana*. The tribes on the North American plains referred to it as *x'iopini*. Today we might call it purpose, mission, or calling, but perhaps the best name would be power. Our purpose in life, the specific difference in the world that we are best suited to make, both in antiquity and today, is expressed in this universal experience of power.

Twenty years ago, when I began to study power, little was

known scientifically about how power influences an individual's interior life. Nor was much known about the experience of powerlessness. I came to realize, though, that knowing what power does to our thought and feeling would help explain the power paradox, and how to outsmart it.

To chart the experience of power, I have studied what it feels like to be placed in positions of authority. I have measured the emotional tendencies of people occupying higher-ranked positions in groups. I have studied the social dynamics of friends and romantic partners, where one individual feels more powerful than the other. I have surveyed people at random times during the day, and captured how they think and feel in the moment, when sensing themselves to be powerful. These studies converge on the notion that power does indeed feel like a vital force. It surges through the body, propelling the individual forward in pursuit of goals.

In more specific terms, when an individual feels powerful, he or she experiences higher levels of excitement, inspiration, joy, and euphoria, all of which enable purposeful, goal-directed action. Feeling powerful, the individual becomes sharply attuned to rewards in the environment and quickly grasps what goals define any situation. At the same time, surges of power make him or her less aware of the risks that attend any course of action. For example, in one study participants feeling powerful were more likely to take risky gambles in a blackjack game that were unjustified by the cards they were holding.

This experience of power propels the individual forward in one of two directions: toward the abuse of power and impulsive and unethical actions, or toward benevolent behavior that advances the greater good. The abuse of power is costly in every imaginable way, from declining trust in the community to compromised performance at work to poor health. By contrast, when individuals use their power to advance the greater good, they and the people whom they empower will be happier, healthier, and more productive. Moreover, this choice allows the individual to enjoy enduring power, which requires that we harness the good feelings of power through a specific set of social practices. The key to enduring power is simple:

> *Stay focused on other people. Prioritize others' interests as much as your own. Bring the good in others to completion, and do not bring the bad in others to completion. Take delight in the delights of others, as they make a difference in the world.*

In the natural state experiments we considered in the last chapter, it was the individuals who were kind and focused on others who enjoyed enduring power in schools, workplaces, and military units, avoiding the fall from power that is so common in human social life. That enduring power derives from a steadfast focus on others makes sense in light of what we have learned thus far: groups give power to individuals who advance the greater good, and they diminish the standing of those who stray from this principle (Principles 5 through 8).

Staying focused on others is supported by the next four power principles, which summarize universal practices that have deep origins in the collaboration and cooperation required of the groups that thrived during our hominid evolution.

> ### Enduring Power Comes from a Focus on Others

PRINCIPLE 9   Enduring power comes from empathy.

PRINCIPLE 10   Enduring power comes from giving.

PRINCIPLE 11   Enduring power comes from expressing gratitude.

PRINCIPLE 12   Enduring power comes from telling stories
that unite.

A first source of enduring power is to focus on what others feel. Practice empathy. Look and listen for the rich language of emotional expression in your social life. In doing so, you will navigate daily interactions in much more sophisticated ways that enhance the greater good.

A second source of enduring power is to give to others. There are many rewards we can provide to others, from the tangible (food) to the symbolic (money) to the social (respect). In sharing such rewards, we will find enduring power, for the beneficiaries of such generosity give power to those who share. One of the oldest ways humans reward others is through encouraging touch, which illustrates how enduring power is found in giving.

A third path to enduring power is to practice gratitude. By expressing gratitude to others, for what they do and who they are, we dignify them. We give them the most cherished reward: being esteemed. Expressions of gratitude provide opportunities for building enduring influence and strong ties.

A final path to enduring power is to tell stories that unite others in common cause. Telling stories is a human universal when it comes to entertainment, to the transmission of knowledge, and to the strong ties and sense of camaraderie that are vital to making a difference in the world.

In every interaction we have the opportunity to practice empathy, to give, to express gratitude, and to tell unifying stories. These practices make for social interactions among strangers, friends, work colleagues, families, and community members that are defined by a commitment to the greater good, where the benefits people provide one another outweigh the harms they cause. Over the course of our hominid evolution, these social practices built social networks characterized by greater trust and better performance. These practices not only benefit those we direct them to; they are inherently rewarding as well, providing some of the most gratifying experiences of having power. They are the quotidian means by which we make a difference in the world.

ENDURING POWER COMES FROM EMPATHY

Thurlow Weed was one of the great political strategists of his day, overseeing the career of William Seward, longtime senator from New York and odds-on favorite to win the Republican nomination in 1860. At the convention in Chicago, Weed worked with his usual focus and verve, visiting the delegates of different states in their hotel rooms, shoring up support. The numbers were looking good. Celebrations were planned. Speeches were being crafted. Had Seward secured the nomination, it would have been the culmination of a distinguished career in politics and public service. But over the course of the night, the political tides shifted, and on the third ballot a young, relatively unknown lawyer, Abraham Lincoln, pulled off the upset. It was a crushing blow to Seward. It was the greatest disappointment in Weed's life.

Lincoln's power is recognized by many historians as the most enduring that we have seen from a president of the United States. Later Weed reflected on him, "His mind is at once philosophical and practical. He sees all who go there, hears all they have to say, talks freely with everybody, reads whatever is written to him."

Lincoln's philosophical genius was rooted in the practical, in knowing the minds of all others. His enduring power lay in understanding what other people felt.

We understand what others feel by carefully attending to the emotional expressions that make up social interactions in daily life. People express emotions in fleeting contractions of facial muscles, shifts in vocal tone, postural movements, tilts or bows of the head, gestures, micropatterns of gaze, and touch. These expressions of emotion are fast, typically lasting only a second or two, but they structure how people relate to one another. Emotional expressions provide information about people's feelings, intentions, and moral judgments of the situation at hand. When a colleague shows signs of anger—with tightened lips, furrowed brow, and slightly raised upper eyelid—I learn that he or she is frustrated, is appraising the current interaction as unfair, will likely act antagonistically, and may feel a sense of righteous indignation.

Emotional expressions evoke specific reactions in others. A

saddened vocal tone or a dramatic call of distress triggers pangs of sympathy in others, increasing the likelihood of supportive behavior. Brief expressions of anger, even those as fleeting as half a second, automatically trigger feelings of fear, weakness, and fight-or-flight physiology in the recipient.

Finally, emotional expressions serve as incentives in social interactions. Warm smiles, vocal expressions of interest, and encouraging pats on the back are all powerful rewards that motivate the recipients to act in specific ways. Conversely, a pinching clasp on the arm or an angry outburst will deter others from continuing the action that precipitated the anger. Emotional expressions, then, structure our daily interactions through the information they provide, the reactions they trigger, and the incentives they represent.

When we are attuned to the expressions of others, as Lincoln was, we engage in social interactions that enhance the greater good. Paying careful attention to others' emotional expressions is a way of showing respect and eliminates some of the misunderstandings and stressful conflicts that can undermine smooth and productive social interactions. It predicts better conflict resolution between romantic partners and more productive negotiations at work.

Practicing empathy also creates a shared awareness of what others are feeling, which is a form of power, freeing people up to respond with greater calm and flexibility to others' emotional displays. When a person in a negotiation expresses anger, she is more likely to get her way, because expressions of anger trigger unconscious reactions of fear and submissiveness in others. Simply paying attention to her expression of anger, and labeling it with words, quiets the fear-related regions of the brain, enabling the individual to handle the anger with perspective and poise.

In a recent study of how well teams performed on collective intelligence tasks, participants were organized in groups of two to five. They reasoned through practical intelligence tasks—for example, identifying what five things a person would need to survive alone in a desert. They tackled tasks requiring logical reasoning. They engaged in open-ended brainstorming. Some of the groups performed better than others. The high-performing groups were the ones led by high-empathy individuals who focused on others' emotions, asked questions, conveyed interest with subtle affirmations and head nods, and adroitly coordinated more sophisticated collaborations. As the proportion of women in the groups rose, notably, so did the team's performance on these collective intelligence tasks. Having more women in positions of leadership is likely to increase innovation and the bottom line.

Empathy, by creating more collaborative interactions, leads people to enjoy enduring power. The studies that support this claim have assessed empathy according to how well people recognize specific feelings from images of facial expressions. In my Berkeley lab, I use this kind of test: first read the emotion words and definitions, then label each face with one word.

▶ *Match each facial expression to
an emotion:*

1. ANGER   feeling offended, opposed, or treated unfairly

2. EMBARRASSMENT   feeling discomfort resulting from
   one's violation of a social norm

3. FEAR   feeling a sense of threat, danger, or uncertainty

4. INTEREST   feeling captivated and fascinated by
   something

5. PRIDE   having a high sense of one's own self-worth

6. SADNESS   feeling grief, disadvantage, loss, and/or
   helplessness

7. SHAME   feeling inadequate, dishonored, and/or
   disgraced

8. SURPRISE   experiencing unexpectedness

If you got seven or eight right, you'd be deemed a high-empathy individual.

So powerful is our tendency to empathize, to attend carefully to the expressions of others, that we even respond empathically to cartoons of emotional expressions. The drawings of the following expressions were made by illustrator Matt Jones, a collaborator of mine. Take a look at the words first, and then match each drawing with one emotion term.

Admiration

Awe

Coyness

Disagreement

Embarrassment

Gratitude

Guilt

Maternal Love

Sadness

Sympathy

Answer key: 1. Coyness 2. Admiration 3. Gratitude 4. Disagreement
5. Sympathy 6. Awe 7. Embarrassment 8. Guilt
9. Maternal Love 10. Sadness

Getting nine or ten right would qualify as a high-empathy score.

Empathy tests measure the kind of sensitivity to other people's emotions and expressions that Thurlow Weed observed in Abraham Lincoln. For people of all ages and in different social contexts, a sharp focus on other people's emotions is essential to achieving enduring power. A high-empathy five-year-old reported having dense networks of good friends when she was assessed at age eight, and she enjoyed greater status in the eyes of those friends. High-empathy adolescents have more friends and are trusted more by those friends and fare better academically. As college students, those who are attuned to the emotions of others do better in school; they are less vulnerable to depression and anxiety and more satisfied with life.

Empathetic young adults moving into the workplace report higher levels of job satisfaction: they prove to be better negotiators, haggling in negotiations that create better outcomes for both sides. Again, the skills that enable us to enhance the welfare of others bring about greater power. High-empathy individuals do better work in their organizations, as assessed by their supervisors. They rise to positions of increased power, and they empower their colleagues. Team members led by empathetic managers work in more productive, innovative, satisfying ways and are less likely to feel stressed and to suffer from physical pain.

We can increase our empathy in so many ways. We can ask open-ended questions. We can listen actively and empathically, orienting our attention to what others are saying. In group conversations, we can rely on the art of quiet and silence to encourage others to voice their views and to avoid the tendency—so amplified by power—to interrupt. We can make sure to ask others what they would do in any situation before offering advice. We can ask those who might feel they have less power—a work colleague or child—for their opinions. Empathy is a first practice that is essential to achieving enduring power.

ENDURING POWER COMES FROM GIVING

The president of the United States shakes the hands of an estimated 65,000 people every year (about 200 per day). On the campaign trail, candidates' hands are often swollen and reddened from touching the body politic. But something deep is at play in this political ritual: touching, and being touched, is one of the simplest and oldest ways in which people provide rewards to others, a basis of enduring power.

Nonhuman primates spend upward of 15 percent of their waking hours grooming one another. They do so not to find nits or gnats or curb the spread of disease but to provide delight and thereby form alliances. You'll recall from Chapter 2 that Luit relied on grooming to create strong alliances with other chimps and to build his power as he mounted his challenge to Yeroen.

In humans, too, touch is a powerful, direct, and evolutionarily old means of giving to others. A reassuring pat on the back or warm embrace elicits in the recipient the release of oxytocin, a neurochemical that promotes trust, cooperation, and sharing. A soft touch to the arm activates the orbitofrontal cortex, a region of the frontal lobes that represents rewards in the environment and actions to attain them. Warm, friendly touches of appreciation make others feel esteemed, valued, and good. Touch is a powerful incentive within social interactions.

Warm, friendly patterns of touch also calm the neurophysiology of stress—elevated cortisol and blood pressure. Simply holding the hand of a loved one deactivates the stress-related regions of the brain when the person is anticipating a stressful experience such as an electric shock. Babies going through a painful medical procedure cried less when a loved one touched them. Like empathy, the right kind of touch advances the greater good in social interactions, enhancing the rewards that others feel and diminishing their stresses.

Given this science of the rewarding and calming effects of friendly touch, I turned to a favorite pastime—basketball—to test the hypothesis that touch would empower others working together and make for greater collaboration and better performance. The participants in my study were National Basketball Association players. At the onset of the 2008 season, my Berkeley research team began coding all the observed touches in an entire game of every team in the NBA. Over seven months, we coded more than twenty-five kinds of touch, from the proverbial high-fives and fist bumps, to bear hugs and embraces. We discovered that men do a funny thing when they express approval—they rap their colleague on the side of the head with a fist. And as teams got the hot hand and were playing exceedingly well, players leaped into the air for flying hip bumps and chest bumps—

a form of celebration I've tried at Berkeley faculty meetings to little effect. On average, each player touched his teammates for about two seconds during a game. Just two seconds.

But those brief touches mattered, leading the teams to play more cohesively later in the season. My statistical analyses found that the more a team's players touched one another at the beginning of the season, the better the team played at season's end, as assessed by the most sophisticated basketball metrics.

The teams that touched more encouragingly early in the season were more efficient with each possession on offense. They helped one another out more on defense. They set better picks and hustled for loose balls. In the end, the high-touch team won a couple more games during the season, often the difference between making the playoffs and not. Still further analyses found that touch improved team performance, regardless of whether the team was winning in the game that we coded, or how well it had been expected to do in the preseason, or how much money the players were making. Power is found in everyday actions of daily living that encourage and empower others (Principle 4).

Our second finding pertains to the empowering effects of brief touches. Some players touched their teammates a lot, to encourage, reassure, appreciate, and celebrate. Others did not. The players who touched their teammates in these encouraging ways made their teams play better. The player who touched his teammates the most was Kevin Garnett, then with the Boston Celtics. When Garnett shoots a free throw, within half a second of shooting he leans forward for two fist bumps from his teammates on the lines perpendicular to the free throw line; then with one continuous motion he steps backward for touches from his two teammates standing behind him prepared for defense.

The year Kevin Garnett won our trophy for most valuable toucher, the Celtics' motto was *Ubuntu*, a South African ethical concept that elegantly encapsulates the four principles of this chapter that are united by an intent focus upon others. Desmond Tutu says that *Ubuntu* is "the essence of being human. It speaks of the fact that my humanity is caught up and is inextricably bound up in yours. I am human because I belong. It speaks about wholeness, it speaks about compassion. A person with *Ubuntu* is welcoming, hospitable, warm and generous, willing to share."

The touches that we observed on the basketball court had these qualities of *Ubuntu*: they were warm, collaborative, affirming acts oriented to others. That is another way of saying they achieved enduring power by focusing on others. They gave the team wholeness and strength. We empower through subtle, often barely visible acts of generosity.

The empowering qualities of touch illustrate a broader power principle: that in providing rewards to others, we find enduring power. We can do this in so many ways: through sharing, encouraging, sacrificing, affirming, valuing, giving responsibilities, and performing the seemingly incidental touches that make up our social lives. And we can do it by expressing gratitude, which is our next principle of enduring power.

ENDURING POWER COMES FROM
EXPRESSING GRATITUDE

Many people associate the great economist Adam Smith with ideas about competition, self-interest, and greed. In 1776 in *The Wealth of Nations*, Smith theorized about the division of labor, money, barter and exchange, the invisible hand, and the problems of poverty. Seventeen years earlier, though, he had published *The Theory of Moral Sentiments*, in which he grappled with the question of what practices make for strong social communities. Like David Hume before him and Charles Darwin after, Smith proved to be a champion of moral sentiments like compassion and awe. "The duties of gratitude," he argued, "are perhaps the most sacred of those which the beneficent virtues prescribe to us."

Gratitude is the reverence we feel for things that are given to us, things that we sense are sacred, precious, or irreplaceable. What is given might be a thing, an experience, an opportunity, a condition of life, or a person. Critically, it must be perceived as something we did not attain through our own agency or will.

A robust new science of gratitude has learned how beneficial it is for individuals to practice gratitude. In an early study, participants took a moment one day each week for nine weeks to write something in response to the following prompt: *"There are many things in our lives, both large and small, that we might be grateful about. Think back over the past week and write down on the lines below up to five things in your life that you are grateful or thankful for."*

Participants who got into the grateful mindset through this writing exercise reported better health, less stress, and more positive emotions like enthusiasm and savoring, several weeks later, than those who wrote about hassles in life or recent happenings. They reported feeling more trusting of and generous toward others. Gratitude is good for us.

Maintaining enduring power, though, comes from translating this interior experience of gratitude into its outward expression. Much like empathy and touch, expressions of gratitude generate social interactions that support the greater good: the shared benefits outweigh the potential harms and social stresses, which in turn strengthens the ties that make up social networks, setting the stage for achieving enduring power.

Expressions of gratitude originated in our ancestors' food-sharing exchanges. Chimpanzees share food systematically with those who groomed them earlier in the day. They use touch to express gratitude toward those who shared food and to encourage further sharing. And in these trades of food for grooming, chimps build cooperative alliances that resemble strong ties among humans.

We too express gratitude in the most rudimentary form with touch. In the study that provided the first evidence for this claim, two strangers came to my lab in Berkeley and were separated by a large barrier, preventing all forms of communication except touch. The person to be touched stuck his or her arm through a hole in the barrier and waited in a state of anticipation. The person on the other side was then asked to communicate twelve different emotions, one at a time, with brief touches to the other person's forearm. The emotions included gratitude, sympathy, and love. After each touch, the touchee guessed what emotion had just been communicated. The communicator used brief clasps to express gratitude; the touchees were able to detect gratitude about 55 percent of the time, easily distinguishing it from tactile expressions of love and sympathy. (Chance guessing would have produced accuracy rates of one-twelfth or 8.3 percent.)

We express gratitude in many other ways—through e-mails, eye contact, deferential bows, and embraces, and by acknowledging and validating in public what someone has said. And like touch, these expressions of gratitude convey esteem, which activates the reward circuits and safety-related regions of the brain, and calms the stress-related regions of the nervous system.

Through expressing gratitude, we build stronger ties within our social networks. Individuals who express gratitude as groups are forming have stronger ties within the group months later. Teachers who cultivate gratitude practices within classrooms, having students regularly write about their experiences of gratitude, empower students to have better relations with one another and to be more committed to doing well in school. They make a difference in the world by cultivating a social atmosphere of appreciation. In a study of gratitude in my Berkeley lab, I tracked the relationships of young romantic partners over the course of an academic year. In the fall, I captured on videotape the degree to which they expressed gratitude to each other during conversations, then six months later ascertained whether they were still together. Those partners who subtly expressed gratitude to each other during the conversations—for example, by validating their partner's beliefs or by nodding affirmatively at something the partner said—were over three times more likely to be together six months later.

Outward expressions of gratitude are a means by which we stir others to more collaborative and productive action. Consider the effects of grateful touch. When experimenters touch participants on the arm in a friendly fashion, those individuals are more likely to sign petitions and cooperate with a stranger. When teachers encourage students with grateful pats to the back, those students are three to five times more likely to go to the chalkboard empowered, and take a shot at solving a hard problem. What's true of touch is true of the spoken word as well. In one illustrative study, participants helped an experimenter edit some text online. The experimenter then thanked some of them for their work personally and sent others a polite message of similar length but missing the thank-you. Sixty-six percent of the participants who were thanked helped the experimenter with another task compared to 32 percent of the participants who were not.

Expressions of gratitude generate contagious goodwill within social networks. In one of the best studies to date on the viral and empowering qualities of gratitude, participants were performing a task on their computer when it crashed, thwarting their attempts to complete the task on time. Out of the blue another participant nearby (actually a confederate) came to the first participant's rescue and fixed the computer, allowing the first participant to complete the task and leave the experiment in a buoyant state of gratitude. A few minutes later our grateful participant then encountered a stranger in need of some help. The participant volunteered to help out more and gave resources to the stranger.

Expressions of gratitude are indeed a most sacred virtue. Found in acts of touch, in the spoken word, and in recognition that empowers others, they are a daily basis of enduring power.

ENDURING POWER COMES FROM TELLING STORIES THAT UNITE

Abraham Lincoln's rise to power from his childhood in Illinois was fueled not by good looks nor by the advantages of class. He came from a poor background and was known for his rumpled, ill-fitting attire, his lack of schooling in the ways of refinement, and his gangly, six-foot-four frame. He helped the United States navigate its transition out of slavery through inspiring speeches and lofty rhetoric—the unifying power of the spoken word.

He loved stories. In their small home in Illinois, Lincoln's father regularly hosted pioneers as they traveled west, and they exchanged lively stories of westward travels and life on the prairie. Lincoln built a grassroots network and strong reputation by touring small towns in Illinois for innumerable hours, recounting the latest courtroom proceedings to small gatherings of interested citizens. These experiences helped Lincoln hone his capacity for storytelling, which proved to be a critical advantage over his better-funded and more established rivals for the Republican nomination, and which helped him negotiate the fractious politics of his presidency.

Storytelling is a pathway to enduring power. To capture this scientifically, over the course of a weekend in October as the colorful fall leaves decorated the streets, I brought an entire fraternity to my Wisconsin lab, in exchange for making a donation to their favorite charity. The "brothers" came in groups of four. Two members of each foursome had just joined, as "pledges," and the other two were "actives," longtime members of the fraternity who enjoyed, by virtue of their seniority, greater power.

My focus was on teasing, a form of storytelling by which people negotiate the conflicts of group life and indirectly express convictions about the social codes that hold their groups together. To get the four fraternity members to tease one another, I assigned each of them a random pair of initials—A.D. or T.J. or H.F. or L.I.—and asked them to give one another a nickname and tell a story—factual or fictional—that justified it. The nicknames were ones you would expect from the profane minds of young men: Anal Duck, Turkey Jerk, Human Fly, Heifer Fetcher, Little Impotent. Every tease lasted only forty-five seconds or so, but the brothers' obscene tales generated howls of laughter, finger pointing, incredulous head shaking, shoulder thumping, and threats of retaliation.

For the next year, I coded each of the 144 teases in a frame-by-frame video analysis. I analyzed the provocation of each tease, its critical element, in terms of how imaginative the nickname was and how improbable and outlandish the story was. I coded the off-record markers of the tease—that is, the nonverbal elements that signal the tease was meant in the spirit of play, like exaggerated facial expressions, amusing tones of voice, and nonverbal acts that signaled levity (a well-timed laugh, a wink). I combined these measures into an index of each participant's storytelling ability, which I related to the number of times that brother had been nominated by other fraternity members as a candidate for a leadership position. (I had gathered this information prior to participants' visits to the lab.) From these peer nominations, I identified the pledges who were enjoying the beginnings of enduring power in the form of positive reputations (Principles 6 and 7). Their teasing involved better storytelling: its provocation was more imaginative and improbable, and it possessed more off-record markers that signaled playfulness.

This basic finding—that good storytelling leads to achieving enduring power—would recur in many studies. In a study of dormitory reputations (the same one discussed in Chapter 2), Berkeley undergraduates were asked to recount something funny that had happened the past week in the dorm. The more esteemed, respected dorm members (as rated by their peers) told dramatic stories that were judged, by outside observers, to offer provocative, attention-grabbing commentary on the other dorm members' reputations. In my study of sorority gossip, it was the higher-status, more respected sorority members who told more dramatic, edgier stories when asked to convey juicy tidbits of gossip about other members.

Good storytelling is a basis of power in young children as well. Several summers ago I decided to create an opportunity for kids to engage in an unusual form of storytelling at a summer basketball camp. One morning the campers—ages ten to fourteen—went through their morning drills at different baskets in the gym.

One drill, actually our study, was called the pressure cooker. Each camper was given one shot from fifteen feet away (a free throw) that would either win or lose a game. They would have to do so, it was explained, under pressure: before they shot the free throw they would be harassed by a "fan" (actually another camper) standing a few feet away. That fan had ten seconds to taunt in any way that he wanted—with the exception of profanities—to reduce the chances our shooter would make the shot. The "fans" did what fans around the world do when harassing a sporting adversary: they taunted, made faces, jumped up and down, hollered, and waved their arms wildly. The taunting included playful entertainment tropes—repetition ("you're gonna miss, miss, miss, miss"), exaggeration ("you've never made a shot in your life"), metaphor ("brick"), and weird facial expressions and apelike imitations. The more respected, esteemed campers (as rated by the coaches) harassed in more playful, funnier ways that possessed the elements of a good story.

Good storytelling makes for enduring power for now-familiar reasons: it enhances the interests of others and reduces the stresses of group living. It promotes the greater good, generating shared mirth, levity, and joy—all dopamine-rich experiences that build strong ties within social networks (Principle 5). For example, in the fraternity teasing study, the funnier teasing of the more respected pledges generated more intense laughter, and shared laughter predicted how much the four fraternity members liked one another at the end of the study. Contagious laughter and shared amusement unite individuals in the spirit of common cause.

Good stories also put into context and make light of the

quotidian conflicts that are inevitable in group life. Telling a story about a rivalry, disagreement, clash of intentions, or contrast in values situates it within a specific place and moment in time, giving ourselves some distance from it. Within organizations, productive teams often include good amounts of teasing, where group members make fun of others' idiosyncrasies and deviant tendencies, thus bringing into focus the norms that hold groups together as well as the enduring wisdom that to err is human.

Good stories are a powerful tool for making sense of life's more complex challenges and stresses. One line of research on this theme, now spanning several decades, followed participants going through stressful challenges and traumas: students nearing breakdowns during exam week, couples working through a divorce, individuals facing cancer and AIDS, people who are recently bereaved. The participants either described the facts of the event, or they narrated their most intense feelings about their stressful circumstances. On every imaginable measure, narrating the emotions surrounding intense, traumatic experiences yielded greater benefits than coolly describing the facts. It reduces levels of stress, anxiety, and depression. Students' grades go up. People facing disease show elevated killer T cell counts and report better physical health.

In stories, we come to understand the difference we are to make in the world. Our identity and purpose in life are nothing more than the story we tell over the course of our lives. Prominent characters appear regularly—mothers, fathers, siblings, friends, lovers, adversaries, teachers, and collaborators. So do important settings—one's childhood neighborhood, the place in Africa where one served in the Peace Corps, freshman year at Cornell, moving around as a military family. Conflicts and failings are inevitably part of the story—battles with parents, rivalries for affection, distance from a sister, a failed project at work. Dramatic actions and turning points move the story forward—a parent dies young, one is admitted to college, a spouse discloses an affair, one serves in a war, or one loses money in a risky financial adventure. And certain themes revolving around great passions—a passion for justice, a desire to help others, a quest for transcendence, a search for power, creativity—recur throughout the story.

People who tell more coherent stories about their lives, with clear plot lines, characters, themes, and organizing passions, are physically healthier and find greater purpose later in life. To the extent that our stories have narrative coherence and encourage others, we empower them toward similar ends.

LOSING FOCUS AND THE ABUSE OF POWER

The four practices that we have considered in this chapter—empathizing, giving, expressing gratitude, and storytelling—can be found in every social interaction. They are paths to achieving enduring power, whether between peers on a playground or between adversaries in the boardroom. Attaining enduring power is simple in the abstract: stay focused on others.

But the experience of having power also has ancient seductions in its DNA. It is accompanied by rushes of positive emotion. It brims with a sense of limitless opportunity. It narrows a person's focus to rewards, goals, and pleasure. As these power-related feelings intensify, our focus on others fades, shifting to an evolutionarily ancient and loud voice in the mind, one that urgently expresses the need for self-gratification, leading quickly to abuses of power.

The power paradox looms, entering into our daily interactions with alarming ease and alacrity. The experience of power, minus a focus on others, quickly leads to the abuse of power. Rather than empathize with others, we lose touch with what others feel and think. Rather than giving, we take, often excessively and in the absence of any need. Rather than dignifying others with expressions of gratitude, we undermine others in acts of incivility. Rather than uniting with others by telling stories of common humanity, we distance ourselves from those we believe to be below us, in arrogant narratives of our own superiority.

The Abuses of Power

I f Machiavelli's (largely wrong) saying "It is better to be feared than loved" is the most widely known maxim about power, Lord Acton's "Power tends to corrupt and absolute power corrupts absolutely" is a close second.

Lord Acton's thesis has now been tested in hundreds of scientific studies, documenting what brief shifts in power do to our patterns of thought and action, and ascertaining what a privileged background of wealth, education, and prestige does to our social behavior. The evidence is clear: when we lose sight of the other-focused practices that make for enduring power (Principles 9 through 12), Lord Acton's thesis prevails. People who enjoy elevated power are more likely to eat impulsively and have sexual affairs, to violate the rules of the road, to lie and cheat, to shoplift, to take candy from children, and to communicate in rude, profane, and disrespectful ways. Absolute power does indeed corrupt absolutely. The experience of power destroys the skills that gained us power in the first place.

In these findings the power paradox strikes us with full force: the very practices that enable us to rise in power vanish in our experience of power. We gain and maintain power through empathy, but in our experience of power we lose our focus on others. We gain and maintain power through giving, but when we are feeling powerful, we act in self-gratifying and often greedy ways. Dignifying others with expressions of gratitude is essential to achieving enduring power, but once we are feeling powerful, we become rude and offensive. We build enduring power by telling stories that unite, but once we feel powerful, we tell stories that divide and demean. It isn't just dictators, power-mad politicians, kings of high finance, and drug-addled rock stars who are vulnerable to abuses of power; the power paradox can undermine the social life of any of us at any moment. Whether we are at work, out with friends, in encounters with strangers, or with our children, the very skills that enable us to gain respect and esteem are corrupted when we are feeling powerful.

These abuses are about absolute power—unchecked by the collective processes through which groups afford power to individuals (Principles 6, 7, 8). Reputational concerns, the quest for status, and the fear of gossip can constrain the powerful, subjecting them to scrutiny and critique, and holding them accountable for their decisions and actions, making abuses of power less likely.

Absolute power renders us vulnerable to the power paradox because our attention is a limited resource. When I direct my attention to myself, I necessarily lose focus on other people. Should I privilege what I am feeling in the current moment, I will perceive more dimly the feelings of others. Should I concentrate my attention on my own interests, I will be less astute in knowing the interests of others. Should I think solely of my own perspective, I will have less insight into how others see the same situation.

Power makes us feel less dependent upon others, freeing us to shift our focus away from others to our own goals and desires. This simple shift in attention takes us away from the practices that enable us to gain and maintain power.

Power corrupts in four ways:

► The Abuses of Power

PRINCIPLE 13   Power leads to empathy deficits and diminished moral sentiments.

PRINCIPLE 14   Power leads to self-serving impulsivity.

PRINCIPLE 15   Power leads to incivility and disrespect.

PRINCIPLE 16   Power leads to narratives of exceptionalism.

The first casualty of absolute power is our focus on others, a foundation of enduring power (Principle 9). When we experience absolute power, our attention shifts to our own interests and desires, thus diminishing our capacity for empathy—understanding what others feel and think. And as our empathy wanes, so does our capacity for moral sentiments that depend on empathy—

namely, concern for others' suffering (compassion), reverence for what others give (gratitude), and inspiration experienced in appreciating others' goodness (elevation). Power diminishes both empathy and the moral sentiments (Principle 13).

Empathy, compassion, gratitude, and elevation are primary drivers of sharing, cooperation, and altruism, direct paths to our own enduring power (Principles 5, and 9 through 12). Lacking the compass of these ancient moral sentiments, when we are feeling powerful, our actions become more self-focused rather than focused on the greater good. Power makes us more likely to act in self-serving and impulsive ways (Principle 14).

Subtler is the next abuse of power: violating the rules of everyday civility and respect, both of which are critical to achieving enduring power (Principle 11). BBC shows like *Downton Abbey* and the novels of Jane Austen portray the powerful and privileged as sophisticated practitioners of the laws of politeness. They act in gracious ways to honor the ethical notion of noblesse oblige, preserving their standing through generous acts that dignify those below them. But science proves that image wrong. As empathy and moral sentiments fade and self-serving impulsivity rises, powerful people prove to be the main sources of incivility, disrespect, and rudeness in social networks, undermining trust and the fabric of civil society (Principle 15).

Even subtle shifts in power can cause people to act in ways that harm the greater good. But humans are quite adept at explaining away their moral infelicities; it is a gifted capacity of the human mind. Those with rising power and increasing wealth justify their elevated rank, and the abuses that such absolute power brings about, with stories of how extraordinary the powerful are, even how biologically different they are from those who don't rise to the top. These narratives of exceptionalism spread the idea that the powerful are above the laws of ordinary people and deserve the bigger slice of the pie that they are so readily inclined to take (Principle 16).

With these abuses of power, the power paradox reaches its dramatic climax. The very principles by which we gain and maintain power are lost upon experiencing power. Power corrupts the very qualities we need to make an enduring difference in the world, and rapidly slips away.

POWER LEADS TO EMPATHY DEFICITS AND DIMINISHED MORAL SENTIMENTS

Empathy is the understanding of what another person thinks and feels, the discerning of the nuanced thoughts and feelings that arise in another person's brain, that three-pound mass of 100 billion neurons connected in infinitely complex ways. But it is well worth the effort: empathy drives many behaviors that enable us to gain power (Principle 5) as well as many practices—understanding others' emotions, listening carefully, treating others with respect—that enable enduring power (Principles 9, 10, 11, 12).

Achieving empathy depends on taking specific actions within face-to-face interactions. We must look and listen with care, attending to others' facial expressions, vocal tones, and movements of the body and eyes. We must respond physically to others' actions, mirroring their gestures, body positions, and expressions, for doing so increases our chances of knowing what's going on in their minds. We must actively direct our attention to what others might be thinking. And we must seek to imagine how others perceive situations we ourselves are in, for shifting out of our egocentric perspective heightens our empathy. All these face-to-face practices are corrupted by power and wealth.

In a first study on this theme, I looked at whether momentary shifts in power undermine the ability to attend carefully to others' expressive behaviors. Participants first viewed the twelve-rung ladder below.

Then some of them were asked to think for a minute about the people who have the most power, wealth, and prestige in the United States; others were asked to think about the people with the least wealth, education, and prestige—the impoverished and out of work and homeless.

During this brief period, participants inevitably compared themselves to those they were thinking about. Afterward they were asked to place an X on the ladder to indicate what they felt was their own standing in society. Participants who had thought about the richest and most educated and esteemed placed their X lower on the ladder. By contrast, those who thought about the less fortunate placed the X higher. Simple shifts in how we perceive ourselves, in comparison to those at the top of society or those at the bottom, lead to marked differences in feelings of power.

Once the participants had been made to feel relatively powerful or powerless through the ladder exercise, they then took a widely used test of empathy that captures the ability to read

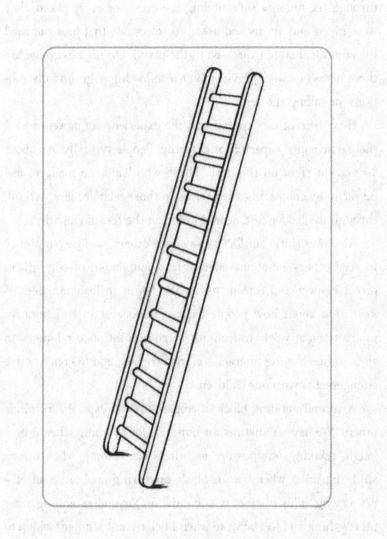

others' emotions by carefully attending to subtle expressions. They viewed a series of photos that conveyed specific emotions through the muscles surrounding the eyes. For every photo, they were given four terms and asked to select one that best matched the emotional state expressed in the photo. On the next page are three items (answers provided on the following page) and instructions for taking the test.

Here as in other experiments, the experience of power eroded the participants' capacity for empathy. People typically get about 70 percent right on this test. Those who had been made to feel powerful by comparing themselves to those who are less well off, through the ladder test, scored lower on the test of empathy.

As power shifts our focus away from others, we lose our ability to read others' emotions effectively, a foundation of why others direct respect and esteem to us. We begin to lose valuable information about how people feel, so important to collaborative interactions at work, to feelings of trust in intimate relations, to smooth functioning interactions with friends, and to constructive engagements with our children.

A second building block of empathy is our capacity to mimic others. We have an instinct for mimicry, for laughing when others laugh, relaxing our posture as others do, smiling when others smile, blushing when friends blush, or tearing up, moved, at others' crying. This instinct is a foundation for understanding what others think and feel because when I behave in a similar fashion to another person, my mind can rely on the feelings generated by my imitative actions to more readily know what that person is thinking and feeling. Taking on the ashamed posture of a friend, the

Look at each of the photos below and choose one term from the four words below the photo that matches the emotion expressed:

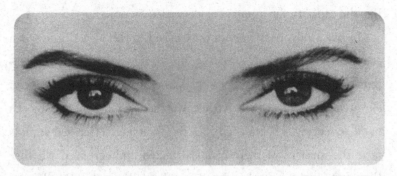

Decisive   Amused   Aghast   Bored

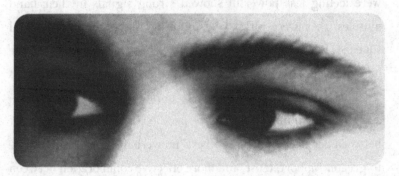

Annoyed   Hostile   Horrified   Preoccupied

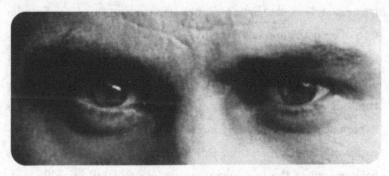

Joking   Insisting   Amused   Relaxed

Answer key: Photo 1 = Decisive. Photo 2 = Preoccupied. Photo 3 = Insisting.

head drop and constricted posture and slouching shoulders, makes it easier for me to understand that person's interior experience. But the capacity for mimicry is degraded by power.

In one study, participants were asked to think of a time when they felt powerful and powerless, an exercise that triggered feelings of greater or reduced power. While experiencing this state of elevated or reduced power, they watched a video of a subject's hand squeezing a rubber ball. As they watched, electrical signals near the muscles of their hands detected and recorded whether they were spontaneously mimicking the ball squeeze. People who were feeling less powerful showed strong signals in their hand muscles: they were reflexively imitating the other person's ball squeeze. But no evidence of mimicry—electrical activity of the hand muscles—was detected in the people feeling powerful.

This short-circuited capacity to mimic others comes with social costs, for mimicry signals respect for others and builds trust between people. Mimicking others' nonverbal behaviors gives rise to greater rapport, trust, and more effective collaboration between teachers and students, doctors and patients, work colleagues, friends, and people flirting. Power undermines this basic foundation of empathy and collaborative interactions with others.

Yet another line of research has documented that social class—a form of power—undermines a third basis of empathy: the active thinking that people engage in when hearing of other people's experiences. The evidence concerned patterns of activation in empathy regions of the brain. Researchers first identified the class background of the participant, according to family wealth, education, and occupational prestige, all of which predict feelings of increased power. Then upper- and lower-class participants read first-person accounts of two personal experiences written by a student of the same gender at their university.

One was about that student's feelings at the start of the semester, and the other was about a recent experience of going to lunch. Focusing on the everyday experiences of others activates the empathy network of neurons in the brain's cortex, which helps us understand their thoughts and feelings. These regions are critical to our ability to imagine what others feel, to understand their thought processes and intentions, and ultimately to adapt our behavior to their actions. The lower-class participants, when reading of another student's experiences, showed activation in this empathy network, but not so for the upper-class participants, whose empathy networks were silent. Coming from an upper-class background, defined by greater wealth, education, and prestige, costs people in terms of their ability to engage in the thoughts and feelings of others, which is a core to gaining and keeping power (Principle 9).

A final path to empathy, and yet another one degraded by power, is taking the perspective of others. This capacity is at the heart of age-old ethical precepts: walk a mile in another person's shoes; see the world through someone else's eyes. The capacity to flexibly move from one's own perspective to the perspectives of others also contributes to more rigorous problem solving, enhanced innovation, more productive negotiations, more sophisticated legal reasoning, and even more effective political discourse. Taking multiple perspectives upon a problem gives us new information and insights, making us more likely to arrive at more sophisticated solutions. And this final basis of empathy—perspective taking—is likewise undermined by power.

In one illustrative study, some participants were led to feel powerful by recalling a time when they exerted control over another person, while others were led to feel powerless by recalling a time when they were controlled by someone else. Then, feeling either powerful or powerless, they performed a simple perspective-taking task: they attempted to draw an E on their forehead so that someone sitting across from them could read it easily. This required drawing the E in the opposite fashion from how they would routinely draw it.

People feeling powerless had little difficulty breaking their egocentric habit and drawing the E to accommodate another's perspective, as seen on the left in the following figure. People feeling powerful, by contrast, were nearly three times more likely to fail at this perspective-taking task. Power deprives us of shifts in perspective out of our own egocentric view, which undermines our enduring power.

Empathy deficits have costs. They make us less likely to benefit from the wisdom of others and less likely to evoke trust in others and gain their esteem (Principle 7). And they make us less likely to experience compassion, gratitude, and elevation. These moral sentiments begin with a focus on others. Compassion arises when we understand the plight of others, and gratitude when we appreciate others' acts of generosity. To be elevated and inspired, we must understand the inner workings of other people's minds and what moves them to inspiring acts of generosity, virtue, or skill. Without empathy, our chances for maintaining enduring

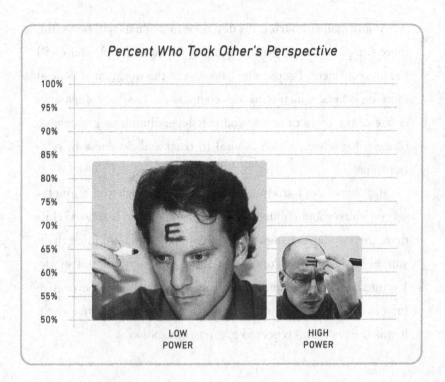

power, and for making a lasting difference in the world, are diminished profoundly.

My tests of these predictions focused first on social class. In a first study, participants reported how much compassion they felt on a daily basis. The finding: the poor reported feeling more frequent and intense compassion for others throughout the day. The reasons are certainly many: the poor are more dependent upon one another to get to work, to care for a sick child (because poverty makes children more sick; see Chapter 5), and to make the neighborhood safe. The poor encounter more suffering in their daily lives, from job loss to chronic pain (see Chapter 5) to hungry children to police harassment and brutality.

At any moment during the day, poor individuals will be feeling more compassion and greater concern for other people than will the more affluent. People who have less in the world must depend more on others, which enhances compassion. Loss of compassion is one of the costs of power and privilege, diminishing our basic concern for others, which is vital to trust and closeness in relationships.

In a subsequent study, students at Berkeley viewed a ninety-second video about children suffering from cancer. It showed children in hospital settings with drawn faces and thinning hair, similar to the image below. My intention was anything but subtle: I wanted our participants to confront some of the most evocative images of human suffering a person might encounter. Once again it was the poor who reported greater compassion.

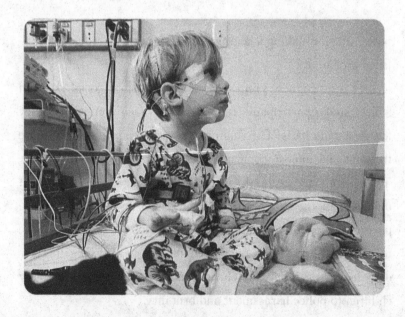

Social class also influences activation in the vagus nerve, the largest bundle of nerves in the body, which evolved in part to support caregiving behavior. The vagus nerve, the riverlike stream from the head to the stomach with a bulb at the end of each "branch" in the drawing below, wanders from the top of the spinal cord to different muscle groups and organs in the body. It stimulates muscle movements in the throat and head, allowing people to focus their gaze on the person in need and to communicate with the face and voice. The vagus nerve also extends to the heart and lungs, allowing for deeper breathing and heart rate deceleration so that people can act calmly on behalf of others who suffer or are in need. Vagus nerve activation leads to increased sharing, cooperation, and altruism—necessities for achieving and maintaining enduring power.

And in the study where participants viewed images of children with cancer, it was those who had grown up poor who showed a strong response in the vagus nerve. Those who had grown up with greater wealth, education, and prestige showed little response in this caregiving bundle of nerves, much as, when considering the thoughts and feelings of others, they showed little activation in empathy-related regions of the brain.

Next I turned to the study of elevation, the feeling of being inspired by the virtue, skill, or noble action of another person. Altruism is a basis for gaining power (Principle 5) and enjoying enduring power (Principle 10), and elevation and inspiration are direct pathways to altruistic actions. When we hear of others' altruistic acts and are in a state of elevation, we are more likely to share resources with a stranger. More generally, elevation and

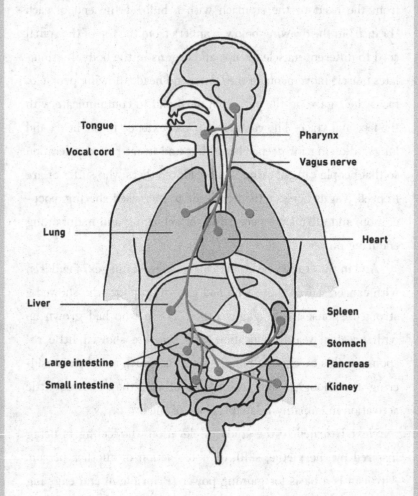

Tongue

Vocal cord

Lung

Liver

Large intestine

Small intestine

Pharynx

Vagus nerve

Heart

Spleen

Stomach

Pancreas

Kidney

inspiration are vital to strong social networks: when people's actions of kindness and generosity move others to enhance the greater good themselves, they are enhancing the trust, goodwill, and cooperation so vital to strong social collectives. But once again feelings of power damage this specific pathway to altruism and enduring power.

In the relevant study, I brought pairs of strangers to the lab: one person in each pair felt more powerful vis-à-vis the other, while the other felt less powerful. The pairs told each other stories about an event that had inspired them in the past five years, like a relative who devoted a life to volunteering, or a friend who risked harm to break up a fight, or a person who started a volunteer organization to help victims of sexual violence. After telling their stories, participants then indicated how inspired and amazed they were by their own story, and how inspired and amazed they felt in hearing the story of the other participant. The person feeling powerful proved to be inspired more by telling his or her own story than by hearing the other participant's story.

You might think this could be due to a difference in the inspiring qualities of the stories—perhaps more powerful people lead more inspiring lives and as a result tell more elevating stories. Not so. A team in my lab coded all stories for how inspiring they were and found no differences in those told by more powerful and less powerful participants. The sounder conclusion to draw is that when we are feeling powerful, we are moved more by our own experiences than by those of other people. The shift in attention brought about by power—from others to ourselves—costs us in terms of being moved by others' inspiring acts.

The costs of diminished empathy and the moral sentiments are considerable. We lose the passions that give rise to the altruism and cooperation that are vital to enduring power. The less powerful are likely to find more powerful people to be disconnected from their concerns (a source of stress that accompanies states of powerlessness that we will focus on in the next chapter). And this corrupting influence of power diminishes perhaps the strongest, most reliable sources of meaning and happiness in life: empathy, compassion, gratitude, and elevation and the acts of altruism they inspire. Feelings of power, by directing our attention to our own desires and interests, actually undermine our self-interest. And most germane to Lord Acton's power-corrupts thesis, this diminishing of the moral sentiments sets in motion a cascade of outward abuses of power.

POWER LEADS TO SELF-SERVING IMPULSIVITY

I first encountered the dynamic relation between self and other focus just as my research on the abuses of power was getting off the ground. I was studying a kind of brain trauma that goes by the name "acquired sociopathy." People acquire sociopathy typically due to a traumatic accident—a car crash, a bike wreck, or falling off a roof—that shakes the head forcefully enough to damage the frontal lobes, the regions of the brain that allow us to empathize and think actively about others. Such accidents can transform upstanding, kind people into garden-variety sociopaths, prone to expressing the purest self-serving impulses. They will make sexual passes at strangers in front of their spouses, shout profanities at their kids, shoplift, go on spending sprees, and have sex in public. As my work on the abuses of power unfolded, I came to believe that experiences of power and privilege are like a form of brain damage, leading us to self-serving, impulsive behavior (Principle 14).

First I studied whether power influences how we eat. I brought together same-sex groups of three undergraduates apiece. A random draw designated one of the three as the group's supervisor, and that person was asked to award the other participants credits based on the quality of their work, which would determine their chances for a cash prize. With this power arrangement in place, the teams dove into their work, writing policies for the University of Wisconsin–Madison regarding academic and social matters. Together they reviewed different sources of information, facts and figures and precedents, and wrote policies for issues such as academic cheating, mandatory tests during senior year, drinking on campus, and university funding of religious groups.

Thirty minutes into their work, the experimenter came into the room and placed a plate of five delicious-smelling chocolate chip cookies on the table where they were working. The plate contained five rather than four cookies, because a law of politeness strongly suggests that we not eat the last piece of food. (When appetizers are passed around at a cocktail party, one last appetizer is typically stranded on the plate and hustled back to the kitchen.) With five cookies on the plate, one of our participants was free to take a second cookie. And indeed the high-power participants were nearly twice as likely to grab a second cookie, with their peers looking on. Recall that their power was randomly assigned, not based on any specific talent, contribution, title, or seniority. Yet the powerful felt entitled to take more.

Eating involves a delicate balance between selfish impulse and a focus on others: reflexive chewing, the opening and closing of the mouth, and the release of saliva are constrained by norms of politeness that remind us not to eat with our mouths open or wolf food down in fist-size bites. Guided by these notions, my research team spent several months coding the videotapes of our participants eating the cookies, focusing on the following indicators of impulsive behaviors:

the degree to which the mouth is open

the number of lip smacks and lip licks

the number of crumbs that fall out of the mouth

When we were finished, the findings could not be clearer: the high-power participants ate more impulsively. They were more likely to eat with their mouths open and lips smacking and crumbs tumbling down onto their sweaters, apparently unconcerned about what others might be inclined to think.

Building upon this result, further studies found that power leads to all manner of impulsive behaviors. For example, sex, like eating, involves striking a balance between acting upon our selfish desires and the interests of others. And in large-scale surveys of nationally representative samples, it is people who have grown up with wealth, education, and prestige who are more likely to express their sexual impulses.

Upper-class children are more likely to play sexual games.

Upper-class young women are more likely to masturbate.

Upper-class young adults are more likely to experiment with nontraditional forms of sexual behavior—oral and anal sex.

Between the ages of 25 and 50, upper-class adults are more likely to be having sex.

In many ways, these are healthy forms of expression, enabled by empowerment. But absolute power can also lead people to express sexual impulses that prove costly to others, such as acts of sexual infidelity. The best estimates are that 25 to 40 percent of men and 20 to 25 percent of women will have a sexual affair during marriage. As pleasurable as sexual affairs are, they are a primary reason for divorce, which is now considered one of the five or six risk factors that predispose developing children to emotional, social, and academic difficulties.

One team of scientists gathered 1,275 questionnaires that had been submitted anonymously by employees of Dutch organizations. The participants indicated their own rank in their organizational hierarchy by placing an X on a six-centimeter vertical line, with 0 at the bottom, which signified the lowest possible rank, and 100 at the top, which signified the most powerful. Embedded in the questionnaire of more than two hundred items, participants indicated whether they intended to have a sexual affair, and whether they had already had one. The more powerful individuals were more likely to admit the intention to have a sexual affair, and they walked the talk as well: 26.3 percent had cheated on their spouses, and the unfaithful were mainly people with power, both men and women.

The simple concept of power leads people to endorse more impulsive, unethical behavior, apparently neglecting the effects of their actions upon others. In studies that get people to think about the concept of power in different ways, participants encountered power-related words such as *boss, rich,* or *authority,* as they unscrambled strings of words and ordered them into actual sentences, as in the following examples:

getting rich richer keep the

playing my golf is boss

more and all we freedom want power

Or participants might simply recall a time when they had power. The transient experience of power produced through these means increased participants' endorsements of unethical actions. People feeling powerful were more likely to say it's okay to not pay taxes, and that there's nothing wrong with overreporting travel expenses or speeding on highways. When we have power, our morals begin slipping away. Power-related moral lapses are not only costly to society; they are also a primary reason that powerful people lose the respect and esteem of others (Principles 5 through 8), a foundation for enduring influence.

I then tested the hypothesis that it would be the rich and not the poor who behaved more impulsively and unethically. The first lab was a California roadway. Between three and six p.m. on a couple of afternoons, two of my assistants were positioned out of sight near a four-way stop in Berkeley. At four-way stops, drivers arrive from four different directions, then, according to their best judgment, allow those who arrived earlier to continue on their way first. The two assistants watched cars approach the stop sign, then noted whether each driver, after coming to a stop, waited his or her turn or cut in front of a driver who had arrived earlier—a violation of California law. The assistants also classified the status of the cars on a one-to-five point scheme based on make, prestige, and age. What follows is a representation of our automobile status scale and the findings.

At the far right is listed the Mercedes, which costs about $130,000, about twice the average annual income of an American middle-class family, which hovers near $67,000. This car is ranked 5 on our scale. Next is a brand-new Honda Accord, ranked 4, then a thoroughly middle-class Honda Civic, aptly named to capture the idea that those in the middle class may be most civic-minded, ranked 3. Those driving an older Ford Taurus or equivalent, ranked 2, probably feel besieged by ominous sounds under the hood, the occasional disdain of drivers nearby, and random stops by the police. And the cars at the bottom of the automobile hierarchy—Dodge Colts, AMC Pacers, Ford Pintos, Plymouth Satellites, Yugos, and other beaters—are a 1 on our scale.

	1	2
	OLD DODGE COLT	OLDER FORD TAURUS
Cut in front of other drivers at four-way stop	7.7%	6.1%
Cut in front of pedestrian	0%	28.6%

> 3 <	> 4 <	> 5 <
HONDA CIVIC	BRAND NEW HONDA ACCORD	MERCEDES
13.1%	9.5%	29.6%
31.1%	44.4%	46.2%

We found that 12.4 percent of drivers arrived at a four-way stop later than other drivers but cut in front of them. And drivers of the highest price-tag cars—those ranked 5—were nearly four times more likely than people driving cheaper cars to arrive later but cut in front of another driver. The wealthier drivers felt more entitled to break a rule of the road.

In a next study I upped the ante. My team positioned an undergraduate at a pedestrian crosswalk on the busiest street abutting the Berkeley campus. Crosswalks in California have broad white stripes designating that portion of the road as a pedestrian zone, where those on their feet have the right of way. In the California 2012 vehicle code handbook, Law 21950 states that drivers must stop and let pedestrians cross before proceeding. It is common courtesy as well.

Right-of-Way at Crosswalks

21950. (a) The driver of a vehicle shall yield the right-of-way to a pedestrian crossing the roadway within any marked crosswalk or within any unmarked crosswalk at an intersection, except as otherwise provided in this chapter.

In the study, an assistant standing out of view verified that each driver of an oncoming car saw the pedestrian waiting at the crosswalk. The assistant made sure there were no other cars nearby; just the driver of interest was speeding toward the pedestrian, who had the law on his or her side. Once again wealth predicted who violated the law. None of the drivers of the cheapest cars—those ranked 1 on our scale—ignored the pedestrians. But drivers of our wealthiest cars did so 46.2 percent of the time. Again, privilege prompts self-serving impulsivity, even at the expense of others' welfare, common sense, and the law.

These findings led me to wonder whether the wealthy would also prove to be more impulsive and unethical in the controlled confines of the lab. In a first study, I had participants complete a widely used measure of social class—the ladder rank measure, marking an X on the twelve-rung ladder you saw earlier, to identify where they fall in the U.S. class hierarchy. Several days later they played a gambling game, pressing a key on a computer that rolled virtual dice. They played this virtual craps game five times, then reported the outcome of their rolls to the experimenter, which determined their chances of winning $50. Unknown to the participants, the roll of the dice was rigged so that the sum of five rolls always totaled twelve. The measure of interest was whether participants report higher scores than twelve. It was the rich who were more likely to lie, reporting higher scores.

Let's cast this last finding within an economic perspective, and its cool calculus of incentives for lying in a game with a cash prize at stake. If I have $100,000 in my bank account, winning $50 alters my personal wealth only trivially. It just isn't a big deal. But if I have $84 in my bank account, winning $50 not only changes my personal wealth significantly, it also matters in terms of my quality of life—the extra $50 changes what bill I might be able to pay, what I might put in my refrigerator at the end of the month, the kind of date I would go out on, or whether I could buy a beer for a friend. The value of winning $50 is greater for the poor, and, by implication, the incentive for lying in our study is greater. Yet it was our wealthy participants who were more likely to lie for the chance of winning fifty bucks.

In the next study, I returned to eating, offering candies instead of cookies that were there to be grabbed. Using the twelve-rung ladder, participants first compared their own class either to the poor or to the very wealthy, which as we have learned elicits feelings of power or powerlessness. Participants completed a variety of other tasks, then were free to leave the lab. As they departed, they walked past a bowl full of forty or so wrapped candies. On the side of the bowl was a label in bold letters:

FOR THE CHILDREN OF IHD

At the Institute of Human Development (IHD) at the University of California, Berkeley, scientists study infants and toddlers and their parents—you can often see them wandering the halls of my department. And yes, in departing my lab, participants who were feeling powerful took nearly twice as much candy as those who felt less powerful. This candy that was meant for the children of IHD. Simply thinking we are above others triggers more unethical behavior.

When these findings were published, impassioned e-mails came flowing in. Some people were enraged and sent expletive-filled missives, railing against Berkeley communists, welfare queens, immigrants ruining the United States, and halfwits and sociopaths in prison. But more told me tales of the ethical lapses of the wealthy: contractors who couldn't collect from well-to-do clients, police officers being lectured by drivers of BMWs after pulling them over for traffic violations, and wealthy clients who never said thank you or who failed to tip during the holidays. Financial advisers to the superrich, and assistants to CEOs, told me about the outrageous ethical lapses they had observed.

Other scientists would e-mail, noting similar findings in their studies. Between 2001 and 2002, researchers surveyed more than 43,000 adults in the United States, seeking to identify the profile of a shoplifter. In the early 2000s, U.S. shoplifters took about $13 billion in goods from retailers each year, and 11 percent of Americans confessed to the act. Themes of power were present in the data: whites were more likely to shoplift than Asians, Latinos, and African Americans. And yes, the wealthy were more likely to shoplift than the poor.

That power leads to self-serving impulsivity is a human universal, transcending cultures, codes, religions, and morals. In one study, more than 27,000 working adults in twenty-seven different countries were asked how often it's justified to: (1) claim government benefits to which you are not entitled; (2) avoid paying a fare on public transportation; (3) cheat on taxes; and (4) accept a bribe. The participants also rated their income on a ten-point scale. Wealthier participants were more likely to say it's okay to engage in the four unethical acts.

The unethical tendencies of the powerful are costly: the more the wealthy participants from a particular country endorsed unethical behavior, the lower that country's well-being. As we rise in rank and see ourselves as above the law and freely gratify our desires, those around us pay a price. The power paradox has steep costs.

POWER LEADS TO INCIVILITY AND DISRESPECT

When Gloria Steinem started *Ms.* magazine in the 1970s, she recruited magazine guru Clay Felker to be its first editor. Felker knew he would risk many things—money, his reputation, the careers of writers he cared about—to edit the magazine. So he insisted on two things: he must have absolute editorial control over the content of the first issue; and the writers—mainly women—must limit the use of obscene language. As women became empowered by the feminist movement, their speech had become unusually profane.

In speech, as in eating, having sex, driving, lying, and cheating, power makes us more impulsive and less attentive to how our actions affect others. Every time you say something, you balance your impulse to express your ideas immediately against your appreciation of your listeners and your anticipation of what they might think and want to say. In just about every imaginable way, gaining power alters this balance, inclining us to communicate more disrespectfully and rudely.

People feeling powerful are more likely to violate the laws of cooperative communication. They are more likely to interrupt others. The rule of taking turns ensures that everyone gets to contribute to a conversation, but people feeling powerful are more likely to speak out of turn. Politeness requires that we express ourselves indirectly, delicately, and with self-deprecation to convey our respect to others, but when we feel powerful, we are more likely to violate such rules of kind speech. We are more imposing in our requests. Our declarations are more direct. Our comments, criticisms, and feedback may be too sharp-edged. Noting a friend's lack of exercise and expanding girth, we are less likely to say, *Have you thought about making it to the gym more often?* and more likely to wisecrack, *Hey, check out the Pillsbury doughboy!*

By contrast, those feeling less powerful are nimbler practitioners of respectful, kind speech. When listening to others, they are more likely to emit what linguists call back channel responses, the *ohs* and *hms* and *ahs* that signal interest in what a person is saying. They are more likely to apologize when making requests. When stating a critique or concern to others, they tend to use softening phrases and indirectness, such as *You might think about . . .* or *I wonder if it would be better to . . .*

Power produces not only less respectful language but also flat-out rudeness. In a survey of eight hundred employees in seventeen industries, about 25 percent reported witnessing incivility on a daily basis at work. Not once a week or once a month, but every day. Employees routinely see others (or themselves) being insulted with profanity. Colleagues routinely tell others that their work is crap, their idea is bullshit, or they are chickenshit. They also fail to listen to others. And people in positions of power are three times more likely to perpetrate such rudeness than those on the lower rungs of the organizational ladder.

The social fabric that is so vital to our sense of trust and

goodwill is built on the moral sentiments that power diminishes—
empathy, compassion, gratitude, and elevation. Absolute power
shifts the individual's attention away from others and toward self-
gratification. It undermines the everyday ethics of social life—
consideration, appreciation, civility, and respect. Quotidian acts of
incivility violate sacred rules of respect, raise people's blood pressure, and undermine collaboration, concentration, and the spirit
of common cause. Through the power paradox, the social fabric
wears thin.

POWER LEADS TO NARRATIVES OF EXCEPTIONALISM

Our tour of the abuses of power reveals that when it comes to
ethical behavior, it is the wealthy and powerful who don't play by
the rules. They are more likely to grab food, express sexual impulses, drive recklessly, and lie, cheat, and communicate rudely.
They disregard social rules at the expense of others and the
norms that bind people to one another. As they move through the
day, they likely leave a wave of everyday social injustices in their
wake.

But people show no shortage of imagination when it comes to
explaining away injustices. For example, to preserve their belief
that the world is just, people will blame victims of rape for the
violence perpetrated on them. To explain why poor people don't
make enough money to get by, others will stereotype them as lazy
and incompetent, even though the typical poor person is estimated
to work at, on average, 1.2 jobs.

When it comes to the injustices that we ourselves perpetrate, our power makes us quite adept at rationalizing such acts so that we can preserve the belief that we are moral, ethical agents. Our power blinds us to our own unethical actions. On this, studies find that people who feel powerful are more likely (a) to admit that they would engage in unethical actions, such as speeding to make a meeting, (b) to state that it's acceptable for them to commit such unethical acts, but (c) to condemn other people for committing the very same unethical acts.

When we feel powerful, we will readily come up with reasons for why it's okay to take resources from our workplace for personal use, but when other people engage in the same unethical act, we just as readily rise in righteous indignation. Power makes us blind to our own moral missteps but outraged at the same missteps taken by others.

These minor forms of rationalization and blame are part of a bigger story that I will call narratives of exceptionalism. The human mind justifies inequalities of wealth and power, indeed any social rank that places some above others, with stories about the unique and extraordinary qualities of those at the top.

For the past thirty years, the income gap in the United States has been rising, and I became interested in how wealth and power bias us toward certain explanations of that gap. Social inequalities require stories to account for the fact that some people are paid millions and others minimum wage, to explain why some children go to schools that look like castles and others go to schools that resemble prisons, why some people rise to the top and others remain below. In a first study, I showed participants a graph por-

traying changes in average U.S. family incomes over thirty years
After the participants studied the graph, I asked them to explain
what the graph portrayed: that the increases in wealth have gone
to people at the top while the wealth of 90 percent of Americans
has flat-lined. Those from upper-class backgrounds were more
likely to attribute the income gap to talent, genius, effort, and hard
work—individual characteristics. The less wealthy, by contrast,
explained it in terms of broad social forces: educational opportunities, political lobbying, and the neighborhoods people grow up in.

The next study asked participants to explain different life
events. Why do some people get divorced? Win an award at work?
Get laid off from a job? Suffer disease? Were such life events due
to the characteristics of the individual—talent, effort, genius, and
character—or to broad social factors? Again, people from upper-
class backgrounds attributed these fateful events to the individual's
talent, effort, genius, and character. In their minds, unique talents
(or the lack of them) determine the course a person's life takes, their
success or failure, their marriage, even illness. By contrast, participants from lower-class backgrounds indicated that the good
and bad events in life are due both to individual qualities and to
forces in the environment.

In every culture, people with power and wealth have told
stories to explain why some people prosper and others don't—
narratives of exceptionalism. Some five hundred years ago, the
British aristocracy enjoyed extremely high levels of wealth, political power, and control over others' lives. And their stories told
of the virility of wealthy aristocratic men, of their heroism in battle (this was when the wealthy fought in wars), and of their keen

instincts in the foxhunt. Such tales helped explain why they lived in vast estates, enjoyed extravagant food and balls, were the fitting choice for maidens, and owned serfs and servants, whom they often abused to gratify their impulses.

During the Victorian era, the well-to-do invoked survival-of-the-fittest theorizing to explain why some individuals prospered and others did not, why some cultures seemed more sophisticated than others, and why some races were superior to others. Wealthy English people fared very well in these social Darwinist narratives of exceptional societies and cultures. Their culture was the most evolved; others were "savage" or "primitive" and lagging immeasurably behind in moral and cultural evolution.

Narratives of exceptionalism have evolved over history, but they persist as frames for making sense of how the powerful and wealthy fare better than others. Had I been alive at the turn of the twentieth century, I might have done as many social scientists at elite universities did and joined the American Breeders Association, then chaired by David Starr Jordan, president of Stanford University. This organization was charged with figuring out "the value of superior blood and the menace to society of inferior blood." The eugenics movement used the IQ test to make sense of superiority; classifying low scorers as "morons" or "imbeciles," it deemed them as threats to the advance of culture. Basing their views on IQ test scores, leading voices in eugenics argued for sterilization of "morons" and "imbeciles" for the betterment of the species and society.

Today in most contexts people do not refer to superior races or savage cultures, but narratives of exceptionalism are alive and well. In my research on how the wealthy and poor make sense of social hierarchies, I asked participants to indicate their beliefs about whether the rich and the poor differ in biologically based ways. Do they differ genetically? Do they have different temperaments across cultures—that is, do those who succeed in different countries have a similar biological makeup? Do rich and poor children differ right out of the gate in biological temperament—is having what it takes to become wealthy and powerful innate? If you encountered two people, one rich and one poor, and they were wearing the same clothing, would you know that they were rich or poor?

I found that the wealthy, more powerful participants were more likely to answer yes to all these questions. A person's standing in society, to their minds, is determined by genes and is thus rooted in biology.

Narratives of exceptionalism matter in innumerable ways. People who endorse biological explanations for class hierarchies advocate harsher punishment of people who have violated the law. As a U.S. politician's wealth rises, that policy maker will become more tightfisted in his or her votes on how the government should direct resources to citizens in need, like the 22 percent of children living in families with incomes at or below the official poverty level (in 2013, $23,250 annual income). People from historically low-power groups—women and African Americans—are less likely to enter into academic disciplines where narratives of exceptionalism prevail, where it is believed that a special kind of innate, raw intellect is necessary to succeed. In philosophy, where such beliefs are rampant, only 31 percent of PhDs are women; in molecular and cell biology, which is less subject to such essentialist beliefs, 54 percent of PhDs are women. Narratives of exceptionalism help explain the astounding rise in CEO compensation: "rare talent" and "genius" are invoked to justify extraordinary salaries of tens and even hundreds of millions of dollars a year, when the empirical data actually find nonexistent or minuscule effects of CEO behavior upon an organization's performance.

Exceptional talent, extraordinary ability, and the good genes alleged to produce them provide compelling accounts of the haves and have-nots in society. They help make sense of social hierarchies and the distribution of wealth and opportunity based on lineage, birthplace, or class. Narratives of exceptionalism provide an easier way of thinking about inequality than considering the complex environmental, historical, political, and economic processes that give rise to disparities in wealth. And they are certainly more palatable than stories about the compassion deficits, impulsive actions, incivility, and unethical tendencies of the powerful. Such abuses of power are easier to demonstrate in the lab than are genetic differences between those who rise to power and those who don't.

WARNING SIGNS OF THE POWER PARADOX

Abuses of power are at the heart of the power paradox and of so many problems of social living. When we lose touch with how others feel, cross lines in expressing our impulses, treat others rudely, and tell stories that demean, we have likely succumbed to the power paradox and are letting absolute power undermine our efforts to make a difference in the world. Absolute power does indeed corrupt.

Fortunately, there are warning signs that we are succumbing to the power paradox. When we abuse power, other people experience stress, anxiety, and shame—signs of powerlessness. Failing to attend to these warning signs will only amplify our tendency to abuse power—we will flirt even more inappropriately and tease more aggressively, for example. But keeping an eye on these warning signs is a way to transcend the power paradox. By focusing on the signs of powerlessness in others, we engage our capacities for empathy, compassion, and generosity—the very practices that help us avoid the power paradox and enjoy enduring power.

Staying focused on the signs of powerlessness, then, will help us transcend the power paradox in our own lives. It also sheds light on more general problems that concern us all. A new science of the social determinants of health and well-being is revealing that powerlessness has more to say about today's social problems—poor health, depression, struggles in school, sexual and racial violence, and persistent racism and poverty—than we might ever have imagined.

The Price of Powerlessness

I n 1970, when I was nine, my mother secured a teaching job at Sacramento State University, and so we moved from trendy Laurel Canyon near UCLA to Penryn, a poor rural town in the foothills of the Sierra Nevada. We lived on Kayo Drive in Penryn for eight years, during which time I came to know the preternatural warmth of the poor—the flip side to the abuses of power we considered in the last chapter: the empathy, kindness, generosity, respect, and inclusiveness that the poor live by in response to the harsher material conditions of their lives. On Kayo Drive, front doors were always open, there was always another place at the dinner table, and the children roamed the hilly neighborhood until sunset and their parents' calls.

With my youthful eyes, I could only dimly perceive the costs of powerlessness that were undermining the lives of my neighbors on Kayo Drive. Being poor produces a way of responding to life circumstances that, while warm and giving, is continually vigilant to threat and chronically stressed in ways that harm a person's mental and physical health.

Every day after school I would walk the length of Kayo Drive. At the top of the road, in the first house on the right, lived a family of four. The father, chronically unemployed, suffered from depression, which had carved sleep-deprived dark circles around his eyes. Their son, a classmate of my brother's, seemed to break a bone in his body every year.

Just across the street lived a single man in his fifties. I only saw him once or twice during my eight years in Penryn. He spent his days inside, with shutters drawn. Later in graduate school, I would learn the name of his condition—agoraphobia, the immobilizing fear of going outside.

Next was the home of my best friend, Memo Campos, whose father Willie worked at a local mill and also owned La Cabana, the bar up the road. For any barbecue, birthday, or quinceañera, he would fill the ice chest with soda and beer. He would die of cancer in his sixties. Memo's younger sister, Yolanda, battled leukemia early in life and through force of will lives to this day in a small house next to her mother's.

After that I would pass the three homes of the Skellengers, who had collectively moved to Penryn from Oklahoma. Lorraine, in the middle house, would die in her forties, all 350 pounds of her. Her husband, Jerry, didn't so much battle alcohol as let it deliver him to sleep.

During my years on Kayo Drive, I could not fully grasp the

profound material disadvantages that my neighbors faced. Even further out of my reach was understanding what this sort of inequity means for society at large and, in particular, for its most powerful members. Looking back now, I see that the empowered, those members of society who so often succumb to the power paradox, might learn a great deal from my former neighbors.

Powerlessness and the power paradox cannot be separated. In some ways, how a society does or does not respond to its most powerless people is a direct measure of its vulnerability to the power paradox. Societies are indeed judged by how they treat their most vulnerable and powerless. By attending to the needs of the powerless among us, we can use our power for the good and contribute to society in enduring ways. Power, as we've seen, is about making a difference to others and is maintained by focusing on others. Very often the powerless are those others. Understanding the causes and consequences of powerlessness catalyzes our awareness of others and immunizes us against the power paradox, just as allowing ourselves to be indifferent or blind to the consequences of powerlessness can give rise to the power paradox. Attending both to the plight of the powerless and to powerlessness's causes is the most important step toward outwitting the paradox.

Ideas and polemics abound as to why the poor and less powerful—like my neighbors on Kayo Drive—suffer from poor health and have difficulty making it in society. Much armchair theorizing would have it that the poor don't care about school or making it. They are shortsighted and make bad decisions. They lack the grit to delay gratification and develop bad habits that shorten their lives. More visceral, politicizing theories go several steps further, insisting that the poor and chronically powerless choose to live a life of ease, as "welfare queens," privileging hedonistic pleasure and exploiting government handouts over hard work.

These ideas make no sense whatsoever of my experiences on Kayo Drive. My neighbors cared deeply about family, community, and society. The children wanted good grades in school and tried hard, but they didn't fare well. The parents were very invested in teaching morals to their kids. The parents and the teenage kids worked hard at jobs—in restaurants, at a lumber mill, in construction, at the fry station at McDonald's, in the fruit sheds—that were typically exhausting, mind-numbing, and meagerly paid. It wasn't lack of caring or desire for a life of ease—something else was undermining the lives of my neighbors.

A clue would arrive in the 1990s, when scientists made a galvanizing discovery concerning power and disease. Poring over health data, they noticed that a person's social class—wealth, education, and prestige—predicts his or her vulnerability to disease. With each rung down the class ladder, they discovered, an individual is more likely to suffer from disease and to live a shorter life, to battle hypertension, cervical cancer, and painful arthritis, and to suffer from other chronic illnesses. These harmful effects were observed even after controlling for the quality of individuals' medical care. Something about reduced power gnaws at our nervous system.

This discovery would inspire a science of powerlessness and help explain why my neighbors on Kayo Drive battled unusual health problems and led shortened lives. First, on a daily basis, the powerless are more likely to face threat (Principle 17). My neighbors experienced threat in many forms: older boys bullied smaller, younger boys; the popular girls in school directed mean-spirited teasing at the girls on welfare; racism and homophobia were directed at my friend Memo; teachers at my school subjected the poorest kids to cruel treatment and corporal punishment; and my friends' parents were threatened by inconsistent work and unstable finances. To be less powerful is to face greater threats of every kind, especially from people with more power.

The powerless, attuned to threats of all kinds, are more likely to experience chronic stress (Principle 18). Among primates, subordinate individuals live in a state of perpetual vigilance to threat, as evident in their intense focus on others and their hyperaroused levels of the stress hormone cortisol. The same is true in humans: powerlessness is the most robust trigger of stress and cortisol release. The daily and chronic stresses of my neighbors on Kayo Drive manifested in many ways: unusual anxieties, sleep disruption, short tempers, the need for extra beer or nicotine.

Chronic threat and stress orient the individual toward defense, undermining most other ways of engaging with the world and causing problems with sleep, sex, creative thought, and trusting interactions with others. Chronic threat and stress damage regions of the brain that are involved in planning and the pursuit of goals. The principle is clear: powerlessness undermines the individual's ability to contribute to society (Principle 19). On Kayo Drive, this could be seen in the difficulties kids had sitting still and concentrating, in their bad grades, and in the depressions so common among their parents. Powerlessness robs people of their promise for making a difference in the world.

Threat, stress, and cortisol not only undermine purposeful action, they also negatively affect the body. They wear down the nervous system, harming veins and arteries, the digestive tract, immune response, cells in the brain, and even DNA. Inspired by that galvanizing finding relating power to disease, scientists would generate all manner of evidence justifying our final power principle: Powerlessness leads to greater physical and mental suffering and shortened lives (Principle 20). It explains the unusual diseases and early deaths of my neighbors on Kayo Drive.

The social problems that most concern us today—anxiety, depression, compromised school performance, chronic illness, and poor health—were pervasive on Kayo Drive. To understand their provenance and think creatively about their solutions, we need to think about their connections to threat, stress, and undermined performance—and to powerlessness. To transcend the power paradox, we must stay focused on the price of powerlessness.

▶ The Price of Powerlessness

PRINCIPLE 17   Powerlessness involves facing environments of
                continual threat.
PRINCIPLE 18   Stress defines the experience of powerlessness.
PRINCIPLE 19   Powerlessness undermines the individual's ability
                to contribute to society.
PRINCIPLE 20   Powerlessness causes poor health.

POWERLESSNESS INVOLVES FACING
ENVIRONMENTS OF CONTINUAL THREAT

Over the course of hominid evolution, the human mind evolved sensitivities to threats typical of the African savannah: snakes, insects, mammals with large canines, loud sounds, males on the verge of violence, rivals for sexual partners, and darkness. Today, as a result of this evolutionary legacy, we are slow to realize the significance of twenty-first-century threats: the severe peril of melting ice shelves and warming seas, high-sugar foods, and the absence of physical exercise. And we are less likely to grasp the chronic threats that the poor, the stigmatized, and the less powerful face on a daily basis. Yet as recent science reveals, to be poor and powerless is to face more threats of every kind.

People living in low-income neighborhoods face more threatening physical environments. Levels of lead, water pollution, pesticides, and hazardous wastes are higher in poorer neighborhoods. Poorer people live amid more chronic, louder noise, and their homes are more likely to be positioned near freeways and train tracks, factories, and industrial zones. They are more likely to have their sleep disrupted by the loud, staccato noise of police helicopters or airplanes landing—and we now know that sleep disruption amplifies the sense of threat. The physical conditions of life are more threatening for the less powerful.

When I was in high school, my friends on Kayo Drive and I went out for drives in our hand-me-down cars, and we were routinely pulled over by the police. They greeted us by shining a flashlight in our eyes, then asked questions, searched the glove compartment, and finally gave us warnings, usually friendly, about behaving ourselves. The surveillance and routine persecution I faced as a young male driving a beat-up car pales in comparison to that of young African American and Latino men, who are less powerful due to the legacy of racism. They are disproportionately more likely to be stopped by the police while driving and to be randomly searched, but they receive harsher physical treatment than I ever did. If they happen to be caught with marijuana, they are far more likely than whites to end up in prison and to serve longer sentences than whites for the same crime. And as nonwhites move into adulthood, they will be more likely to face rejection from society's institutions, which directly undermine their capacity to make a difference in the world. When African Americans apply for jobs, potential employers judge their résumés more harshly than comparable résumés submitted by white applicants. When seeking housing, even when submitting applications with the same financial data as other people, African Americans are treated more critically and will have fewer housing options. Society's institutions tend to reject, exclude, and marginalize people whose identities, by dint of history, give them less power.

Those with less power also experience being under represented, or in the numerical minority. Simply being in the numerical minority in a neighborhood exposes people to racial violence, while being in the majority leads people to be more aggressive in impulsive ways (Principle 14).

Power imbalances also produce patterns of violence against women. In more than 150 cultures that have been studied, when women are less well represented in education, politics, and the workforce, they are more likely to be victims of sexual violence and to feel the chronic threat of such violence. Women face sexual harassment in the workplace more commonly when they are less well represented in positions of power there.

Finally, the powerless chronically face the threat of impulsive behavior by more powerful people. At work, when the powerful act out in a rude and arrogant fashion, their subordinates feel more threatened. More generally, when people abuse their power by interrupting others, failing to listen, teasing with hostility, or touching overaffectionately, the targets of such actions, who are almost always individuals with less power, feel threatened.

Poorer children express greater mistrust of adults, school administrators, and other sources of authority because such representatives of society's institutions tend to punish them disproportionately. Children's hypersensitivity to threat extends even to their interactions with peers: if poor kids see a video of one child bumping into another in a lunch line, they will assume that it was aggressively motivated. This hypersensitivity to threat has ironies embedded in it: when lower-class kids were asked to imagine a store clerk walking over to ask how they were doing, they were more likely than wealthier kids to assume that the clerk was doing so to catch them in some kind of criminal activity, even though, as we have seen, wealthier kids are more likely to shoplift.

This chronic sensitivity to threat leads the poor to develop hypervigilant brains, perpetually on high alert, ready to devote the brain's precious resources to detecting and responding to threats. In one study, participants were asked to match a photo of a facial expression at the top of the page with the same expression positioned among a set of three faces presented at the bottom of the page. I've given an example of this task on the facing page.

When the participants were matching the anger expression, those who had grown up in low-income neighborhoods showed greater activation in the amygdala, which triggers further stress-related responses in the nervous system.

People experiencing powerlessness are likely to seem reserved, constrained, and inhibited. People who feel powerless are likely to speak up less, to be constrained in their expression, and to hesitate in taking action. If power makes us impulsive, powerlessness makes us reserved. Some might assume that people feeling powerless are disengaged or worse—uninterested or lazy. But just the opposite is true: powerlessness brings a hypervigilance to threat. The day-to-day experience of threat—discovering lead or mold in a child's bedroom wall, being told no by a series of loan officers, being treated rudely at work—communicates that less powerful individuals have less value than others. In the less powerful, such threats cause the stress response to go into overdrive.

STRESS DEFINES THE EXPERIENCE OF POWERLESSNESS

To understand the biology of social threat—so central to feelings of powerlessness—scientists created the Trier Social Stress Task (TSST). Participants show up, then after ten minutes of preparation must deliver a speech to an audience of strangers on a

Match the face just below to the same face presented in the row of three facial expressions.

topic of the experimenter's choosing—for example, they must argue on behalf of euthanasia or against the role of NSA surveillance in contemporary society. As they deliver the speech, the audience reactions resemble the disinterested tendencies of people succumbing to the power paradox: critical looks, skeptical headshakes, frustrated brow furrows, and *harumphs* and *phuhs* of contempt.

Being threatened socially in this fashion triggers an ancient branch of our nervous system known as the HPA axis, which involves a series of chemical communications between the hypothalamus, the pituitary gland, and the adrenal glands, leading to the release of cortisol into the bloodstream.

Cortisol readies the body for defense and fight-or-flight behavior. It increases heart rate and blood pressure, thereby distributing blood and its nutrients to muscle groups and organs. It triggers the release of sweat in the hands, to aid in clasping and grabbing in adversarial encounters. It activates glucose production, needed to feed cells during metabolically demanding action.

Cortisol also stimulates the immune system, the network of cells and glands that helps the body fight infections and heal injuries. A branch of the immune system, the cytokine system, triggers inflammation responses near damaged tissue. It stimulates other cells to absorb and kill pathogens such as toxins, bacteria, and viruses. And it signals the brain to trigger "sickness behaviors," which include increased sleep and withdrawal. Together these responses help the body recuperate from illness or injury that is more likely under conditions of threat.

Threats that devalue a person's social identity are particularly potent triggers of cortisol release and elevated cytokine levels. They activate the biology of defense. When low-income kids attend elite colleges and sense that their class background is devalued, they show an elevated cytokine response. When female college students read an essay about how pervasive and enduring sexism is, their cortisol rose; when they read an essay about how sexism has plateaued, their cortisol levels did not shift. When African Americans received critical evaluations from whites, they showed elevated physiological arousal consistent with a defensive response.

At work, when we feel disempowered, our bodies respond by increasing cortisol. Research on leaders in the military, government, and the public sector found that those who did not have a say in promotions, salaries, or budget decisions or receive direct reports from others showed higher levels of cortisol. Regardless of title or salary, those who experience less power at work, without a chance to make a difference, have higher levels of stress-related cortisol.

So direct is the linkage between powerlessness and the biology of defense that simply arranging our bodies in a powerless posture elevates cortisol. Study participants who were asked to move their bodies into a position of powerlessness drooped their shoulders and head and clasped their hands when seated—classic expressions of shame and defeat; when standing, they clasped their arms and crossed their legs—movements that diminished their size and physical power (see following page). Those who were asked to move their bodies into powerful postures sat with their arms akimbo leaning back in the chair for a minute or two, then stood with their hands on the desk, leaning in (see below).

Poses of Powerlessness

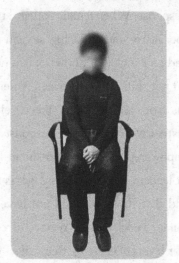

Poses of Power

Simply moving the body into a posture of powerlessness, the researchers found, led to a rise in cortisol. Striking the pose of power, by contrast, led to decreased cortisol and increased testosterone, a hormone that increases status-elevating behavior.

Chronically high levels of cortisol, triggered by powerlessness, have been shown to change the individual's brain, further amplifying the vigilance to threat. Cortisol increases the amount of myelin that covers the neurons connecting the hippocampus, where the sense of self arises, and the amygdala, a threat-related region of the brain. What this means is that stress and cortisol strengthen the neurochemical communication between the threat- and identity-related regions of the brain, amplifying the influence of powerlessness upon the vigilance to threat and the feeling of stress.

POWERLESSNESS UNDERMINES THE ABILITY TO CONTRIBUTE TO SOCIETY

The human stress response is a dictatorial system, shutting down many other processes essential to our engagement in the world. Cortisol suppresses the activity of the digestive system, thus keeping resources available for fight-or-flight behavior. It interferes with sleep and repose, which is not helpful, to say the least, in responding effectively to threat and danger. It sharpens the mind's focus on potential peril and threat, to the exclusion of other stimuli in the environment.

As a result, the chronic stress associated with powerlessness compromises just about every way a person might contribute to the world outside of fight-or-flight behavior. Powerlessness compromises the sexual response, a delicate biological process involving patterns of blood flow and excitement in the sexual organs. A loss of income has been found to lead to sexual dysfunction in women and erectile dysfunction in men.

Powerlessness also has profound effects upon intellectual function. By directing our attention to threats, it enables certain kinds of cognitive functioning—most notably empathy and understanding others' mental states (Principle 13)—but it undermines rigor of thought and quality of decision making. One study brought graduate students together as teams to make a recommendation as to which candidate an organization should hire. One group was led by someone succumbing to the power paradox: the person spoke loudly, frequently interrupted others, and stared and pointed in mildly threatening ways. The other group was led by someone more even-keeled. The threatening leader made the participants feel more fear and stress, and as a result, they made a worse decision about whom to hire: they chose the less qualified candidate that the leader nonetheless preferred.

In another study, participants arrived at a lab to take a standard test of creativity that requires people to solve anagrams and generate novel uses of an object, such as paper or a brick. While waiting for the test to begin, an experimenter lashed out at and dismissed a participant who had shown up a bit late. The participants sitting nearby, reacting to the abuse of power, felt stressed and frustrated and solved one less anagram problem and generated two fewer responses than participants in a control condition.

Recent research is showing that chronic powerlessness—

poverty—stunts brain development in perhaps permanent ways that undermine not only school performance but also the capacity to contribute to society more generally. A team of neuroscientists scanned the brains of more than a thousand children at several points in their lives. Early in life, the brains of poor and wealthier children looked quite similar. But by age eleven, the brains of the poorer children were 5 percent smaller. The regions of the brain that poverty most stunted, such as the parietal cortex, were those that enable language, planning, reasoning, academic work, and regulating stress. Poverty suppresses growth in regions of the brain that empower children to do well in school, handle the greater threats they face on a daily basis, and eventually make a difference in the world.

The prices of powerlessness range from the sexual to the intellectual, influencing every possible way an individual might contribute to the world. It should come as no surprise, then, that powerlessness diminishes a person's sense of purpose and enjoyment of life. Put aside any notion you might have that low-income people live lives of ease and pleasure and that it is high-income people who suffer angst and anxiety. Studies of happiness show that people who experience less power on a daily basis, or who are in low-power positions within a social group, or who live in poorer neighborhoods, are less happy than those with more power. These findings are true of adults as well as of children.

People who face chronic poverty are more vulnerable to clinical anxiety, often accompanied by panic attacks—exhausting, powerful biological reactions to perceived threats and the belief that one is soon to die.

Low-income individuals are also more vulnerable to depression. The poor and less powerful are nearly twice as likely to experience major episodes of depression—extended periods of feeling disconnected, apathy, despair, and the absence of joy and purpose.

It is a myth of power that the well-to-do suffer disproportionately from despair, feelings of meaninglessness, anxiety, and depression. This myth makes for great scenes in Woody Allen's films and *New Yorker* short stories, but it belies the realities of powerlessness.

POWERLESSNESS CAUSES POOR HEALTH

Powerlessness has one final cost: poor health (Principle 20). Ever since that bellwether study linking power to disease, dozens of other studies have portrayed exactly how powerlessness harms people's health. One examined women's health over several months. Controlling for diet, smoking, and other health risk factors, the women lower in social class had worse physical health. They experienced greater difficulties getting to sleep at night. Their hearts beat faster and worked harder, making for dangerously high blood pressure and greater wear and tear on the arteries and veins—a cardiovascular profile associated with greater likelihood of strokes and heart attacks. The women feeling relatively powerless were also more obese in the abdominal region, which is more associated than other forms of obesity with poor health outcomes. Levels of cortisol were higher for the lower-ranked women throughout the study.

Poorer moms, their own health compromised by powerlessness, are more likely to have premature and underweight babies. Those relatively less powerful babies, as they develop into toddlers and then children, are more likely to suffer from every health ailment, from asthma to obesity. As adults, people who grow up poor and powerless are more prone to cardiovascular disease, diabetes, and respiratory illness. Their days are more likely to be shaped by the pains of bad backs, stomach problems, and headaches.

So powerful are the effects of powerlessness upon health that it actually damages telomeres, strands of DNA that hold the chromosomes together, giving stability and strength to the cells. Telomeres shorten with age, contributing to the aging of cells. And a recent review of studies involving hundreds of thousands of participants from over fifteen countries found that less powerful individuals—in terms of social class—consistently had greater shortening and premature aging in their telomeres. Feeling powerless is a fast track to a shorter life.

These damages of threat and stress—the profile of powerlessness—are particularly toxic for young children. Childhood is a critical period for the calibration of the HPA axis and the cytokine system. Young children are busy learning what sounds make up their culture's spoken language, and what tastes make up its cuisine, but they are also learning about the threats and perils in their environment, attuning their HPA axis and immune systems accordingly. Poor children quickly learn that threats of all kinds are pervasive (Principle 17), and chronically high levels of cortisol and inflammation result. People who grew up poor show greater cardiovascular response to threatening stimuli, higher levels of cortisol, and elevated immune system activation and bodily inflammation.

Chronic inflammation and increased cortisol predispose poor children to a rapid onset of different diseases. Plaque buildup in the arteries is more likely, raising the poor child's risk of heart disease. Should a tumor occur, it will grow faster and spread more quickly. In a stressed-out, inflamed state, the poor child is more vulnerable to "frailty syndrome": the bones weaken, he or she will lose muscle mass, and sudden falls from bikes or backyard rope swings or skateboards are more harmful.

Combining all these effects, a child in poverty faces a 20 to 40 percent greater risk of dying by disease, stroke, and cardiovascular disease. Growing up poor in the first quarter-century of a person's life shaves six years off life expectancy. This remains true even if a poor child enjoys upward mobility and, as an adult, greater wealth and prestige. Simply by virtue of being born poor, my friends on Kayo Drive could, on average, expect six fewer years of life and greater health problems of all kinds.

TRANSCENDING THE POWER PARADOX

My parents gave me an interest in science, a love of experiments from the personal to the scientific, an interest in poverty, gender, race, and social class, and a predilection to look critically upon the status quo. Most unexpected of the gifts they gave me, though, was life on Kayo Drive. Not many parents upon obtaining a job would move to a neighborhood where their children's new friends would be less likely to go to college and more likely to lead troubled lives than in the neighborhood they left. But that is what we did. This move—from a well-to-do community to a poor rural town—opened my eyes to the effects of power upon daily life and set in motion my study of the power paradox.

On Kayo Drive I first encountered the price of powerlessness. I learned that the poor encounter more threats of just about every kind, often from people in positions of power, and that these threats lead them to feel devalued (Principle 17). I saw firsthand that these threats lead to stress, compromised performance, and worsened health and well-being (Principles 18, 19, 20)—emotional disorders, poor academic performance, and unusual diseases. Seeing these principles play out in the lives of my neighbors on Kayo Drive drove me to study the power paradox. The findings that that interest led to—the price of powerlessness—are stronger than I might have imagined. Powerlessness is the greatest threat to a person's promise of contributing to society, as well as to their individual health and well-being.

As grim as these findings are, they point to simple and inexpensive ways we can mitigate the price of powerlessness. Reducing the threats to the identities of the less powerful will allow them to fare better; it is good for a society's health and well-being to fight racism, sexism, homophobia, inequality, and other identity-devaluing threats, and to give voice and opportunities to those who have been disenfranchised in the past. Increasing the value that the powerless feel they have in society will allow them to fare better; it pays to do things that dignify the less powerful, that communicate that they are worthy like everyone else. When the less powerful are given simple means to handle the stresses of their station, such as exercise, immersion in nature, or mindfulness techniques, they fare better at school and in their daily living. When green spaces are added to poor urban neighborhoods, or when lead in poor people's homes is reduced, or when kids in poor schools are taught to calm their stress through simple breathing exercises, or when low-income college students form trust-enhancing casual friendships with white students at elite universities, the sense of threat fades and sense of being valued increases, and their health and performance rise.

Just as important, my experiences on Kayo Drive taught me that the effects of powerlessness are pervasive and are typically underestimated. They were evident on a winding rural road in a town far from everything, during a time when inequality was much less than it is today. When we succumb to the power paradox and act in ways that disempower others, we are likely having direct problematic effects on the lives of others. Being aware of the many prices of powerlessness is the most powerful antidote to the power paradox.

Epilogue:
A Fivefold Path to Power

So how can we outsmart the power paradox? What insights can we glean from this new science so that we avoid the mistakes of the past and make the most of our power? The power paradox touches every facet of our daily lives, from family to work to society. It explains what is inspiring in human social life—innovation, sacrifice, discovery, and progress over history—as well as what we are most concerned about bettering—disease, depression, and deprivation, as well as injustice, subjugation, and violence.

Every human seeks to make a difference in the world, to have some form of power or influence that leads to the esteem of others. From one vantage point, societies are patterns of organization that respond to the basic human aspiration to make a difference in the world. The ethical principles that follow are one approach to enabling people to pursue this aspiration. They amount to a five-fold path to enduring power in our daily lives.

1. *Be aware of your feelings of power.* The feeling of power is like a vital force moving through your body, involving the acute sense of purpose that results when we stir others to effective action. The first path to power is to be aware of this feeling. Doing so will help you find answers to one of life's most poignant questions: What is your purpose in life? The feeling of power will guide you to feel the thrill of making a difference in the world.

If you remain aware of this feeling and its context, you will not be entrapped by myths that power is money or fame or social class or a fancy title. Nor will you be held back by the misguided notion that if you are not well endowed in these ways, you cannot make a difference in the world. Money, fame, class, and titles are just symbols, or opportunities, for making a difference. Real power means enhancing the greater good, and your feelings of power will direct you to the exact way you are best equipped to do this.

2. *Practice humility.* Collectives endow us with power: they most define our identities and the reputations that capture and codify them. We feel our power in the esteem others direct to us. We can lose it in stinging gossip that targets selfish, Machiavellian acts. Power is a gift. It is the chance to make a difference in the world. People who excel in their power—the speech therapist who leads children with severe language issues to engage in the world socially, the physician who improves the health of dozens of people a

day, the high school teacher who every day inches her students toward academic success given improbable odds, the family judge who uses the law to maintain ties between families going down in flames, the writer whose piece of fiction or nonfiction stirs others' imaginations, the venture capitalist who funds a game-changing startup, the prisoner who brings peace to the prison yard—they all know this. They feel the rush of dopamine and vagus nerve activation in the purest moments of empowering others and lifting up the greater good. To influence others is a privilege. To have power is humbling.

People who enact their power with humility enjoy more enduring power. Ironically, the more we approach our power, our capacity to influence others, with humility, the greater our power is. Don't be impressed by your own work—stay critical of it. Accept and encourage the skepticism and the push back of others with an open mind, and encourage it. Remember that others have enabled you to make a difference in the world. There is always more work to do.

3. *Stay focused on others, and give.* The most direct path to enduring power is through generosity. Give resources, money, time, respect, and power to others. In these acts of giving we empower others in our social networks, enhancing our own ability to make a difference in the world.

Such acts of generosity are critical to strong societies. Empowered individuals are happier. Mutually empowered individuals in romantic partnerships have better sex and feel more commitment to each other. Mutually empowered parents and children get along better. When neighbors feel equally empowered, they feel greater trust and camaraderie. At work, leaders who create atmospheres of empowerment build organizations that are happier and more productive. More democratic nations—where many are empowered—tend to have healthier and happier citizens.

At every level of analysis, the more we empower others, the more the greater good is increased. So give in many ways, especially in ways that empower. This will prove to be the most important foundation not only of your making a lasting difference in the world but also of your own sense of happiness and meaning in life.

4. *Practice respect.* By directing respect to others, we dignify them. We elevate their standing. We empower them. Respect emerged out of the patterns of mutual deference and sharing in our hominid ancestors and is seen in primates today. That all members of a social collective deserve some basic form of dignity is an ancient basis of equality, and it is expressed in our day-to-day lives through respect.

Practicing respect requires work. There is no reward people value more than being esteemed and respected. Those who have less power are gifted practitioners of respect—praise, compliments, polite language, deferential nonverbal behavior—but the powerful often abandon these practices. So to avoid the abuses of power, and to enjoy enduring power, take this fourth path and practice respect. Ask questions. Listen with intent. Be curious about others. Acknowledge them. Compliment and praise with gusto. Express gratitude.

5. *Change the psychological context of powerlessness.* The four previous paths to power are necessary steps in this direction: being aware of your feelings of power, practicing humility, giving, and respecting are all means by which, in our families, at work, and in our communities, we can minimize the tendency for some people to feel below others, so toxic to health and well-being.

We can do more, though. Should you have the time, pick one price of powerlessness and change it for the better. The rise in inequality and the persistence of poverty give us many opportunities for such work. These problems have economic and political solutions. But there are also psychological solutions to the price of powerlessness—the threat, stress, compromised performance, and poor health that arise when people feel below others. They begin in valuing others.

Attack the stigma that devalues women in society. Confront the racism that costs African Americans in terms of their health and well-being and contribution to society. Call into question elements of society—solitary confinement, underfunded schools, police brutality—that devalue people. And seek change. Create opportunities within your community and workplace that empower those who have suffered disempowerment due to the moral mistakes of the past. This may not feel like the game-changing social revolutions of earlier times, but they are quiet revolutions just the same, and they are very much needed today.

When I was in my twenties, steeped in the utopian idealism of youth, I wished for a society that would be power free. It is a powerful intuition—the desire for equality—seen around the world in people's preferences for sharing resources with others, and for how they would like to see society arranged. My youthful hope was that we would move toward a more equal society, free of power dynamics, status hierarchies, rank of almost any kind, and, it went without saying, subjugation, humiliation, and coercion.

Carrying out the science that led to this book has changed my view. I still am guided by that deep intuition of equality, and I seek ways to reduce stigma, coercion, and the devaluing of people. But now I wish for a society where people—all people—would have as much power as possible, for power will always be present in our social lives. I hope that we can figure out more and better ways to outsmart the power paradox, that basic pattern in human social life and history. Should we do so, we will enable more people to make the difference in the world that they are uniquely suited to make.

Acknowledgments

I have been so fortunate in writing this book to be empowered by such generous and insightful minds. The content of this book took shape in conversations on hikes, in cafés, and in local watering holes with: Arturo Bejar, Jennifer Berdahl, Chris Boas, Nathan Brostrom, Gustave Carlson, Christine Carter, Pete Docter, Deirdre English, Claire Ferrari, Tom Gilovich, Deborah Gruenfeld, Leif Hass, Jeanie Keltner, Natalie Keltner-McNeil, Serafina Keltner-McNeil, Michael Lewis, Michelle Long, Jason Marsh, Mollie McNeil, Dan Mulhern, Richard Nisbett, David Perry, Paul Pierson, Paul Piff, Ananya Roy, Gail Sheehy, Connie Sobczak, Claude Steele, Lee Townsend, and the men in blue at San Quentin State Prison. Several people have provided precious and game-changing input on written chapters, and to you I am so very grateful: Cameron Anderson, Andrew Bacevich, Laura Kray, Galen McNeil, Steve Pinker, Michael Pollan, and Laura Stickney. Books often take many months or years to write but have their origins in fateful moments, and this one began in a conversation with Tina Bennett, my agent, who sensed the necessity of a book on the radically changing nature of power. Thank you, Tina, for your guidance, provocative insight, and strong touch. This book came to fruition thanks to the vision of Ann Godoff. I won't write down the words to express my reverence for her sense of a good argument and clear phrase and how abundantly she passed on her wisdom to me, for she'd need to rework those words, give them some sort of logical structure, and make them zing. All I can say is that it has been a truly exhilarating intellectual journey to see this book take shape with Ann. And finally, this book would not exist without the innovative, burn-the-midnight-oil scientific efforts of my extraordinary collaborators at the Berkeley Social Interaction Lab: Maria Logli Allison, Cameron Anderson, Olga Antonenko, Yang Bai, Jennifer Beer, Belinda Campos, Serena Chen, Daniel Cordaro, Stephane Côté, Matthew Feinberg, Adam Galinsky, Jennifer Goetz, Gian Gonzaga, Amie Gordon, June Gruber, Erin Heerey, Matt Hertenstein, Liz Horberg, Emily Impett, Hooria Jazaieri, Oliver John, Alex Kogan, Michael Kraus, Carrie Langner, Jennifer Lerner, Andres Martinez, Laura Maruskin, Rudy Mendoza-Denton, Chris Oveis, Paul Piff, Laura Saslow, Sarina Saturn, Disa Sauter, Lani Shiota, Emiliana Simon-Thomas, Daniel Stancato, Jennifer Stellar, John Tauer, Ilmo van der Lowe, Gerben van Kleef, Dan Ward, Robb Willer, Randy Young, and Jia Wei Zhang. Without you, I'd be baking bread in some café in Santa Cruz. Thank you all. You have hearts full of napalm.

Notes

Introduction

7   **bouts of mania:** S. Johnson, L. J. Leedom, and L. Muhtadie, "The Dominance Behavioral System and Evidence from Psychopathology: Evidence from Self-Report, Behavioral, and Biological Studies," *Psychological Bulletin* 138 (2012): 692–743.

9   **gap between rich and poor:** Rich Morin, "Rising Share of Americans See Conflict Between Rich and Poor," Pew Research Center, January 11, 2012, http://pewrsr.ch/1NVNw69.

10   **powerlessness, poverty, and inequality:** Jacob Hacker and Paul Pierson, *Winner-Take-All Politics: How Washington Made the Rich Richer—And Turned Its Back on the Middle Class* (New York: Simon & Schuster, 2010).

10   **poverty and racism are persistent:** Joseph E. Stiglitz, *The Price of Inequality* (New York: W. W. Norton, 2013).

10   **power imbalances:** G. William Domhoff, *Who Rules America?: Power and Politics,* 4th ed. (New York: McGraw-Hill, 2001), and *Who Rules America?: The Triumph of the Corporate Rich* (New York: McGraw-Hill, 2013).

10   **"get under our skin":** For a compelling take on the cognitive psychology of powerlessness, see Sendhil Mullainathan and Eldar Shafir, *Scarcity: Why Having Too Little Means So Much* (New York: Henry Holt, 2013).

10   **depression, anxiety, and violence:** Richard G. Wilkinson and Kate Pickett, *The Spirit Level: Why More Equal Societies Almost Always Do Better* (London: Allen Lane, 2009).

12   **many books already:** For example, Walter Isaacson, *Profiles in Leadership* (New York: W. W. Norton, 2010).

13   **"soft power" and "hard power":** Joseph Nye, *The Future of Power* (New York: Public Affairs, 2011).

14   **New economic superpowers:** For excellent discussions of the changing landscape of the power of nations, see Andrew J. Bacevich, *The Limits of Power* (New York: Henry Holt, 2008), and Fareed Zakaria, *The Post-American World* (New York: W. W. Norton, 2009).

Chapter 1: Power Is About Making a Difference in the World

19 **a country's economic strength:** Paul Kennedy, *The Rise and Fall of the Great Powers* (New York: Random House, 1987).

19 **The Prince:** Peter Constantine, ed., *The Essential Writings of Machiavelli* (New York: Random House, 2007).

19 **taught in schools of government:** Although there is controversy about Machiavelli's intentions in writing *The Prince*, the influence of this book is not controversial. It routinely makes lists of the one hundred most influential books ever written, having shaped the actions of some of the most powerful people in history. Robert Downs summarized its place in history thus: "The list of avid readers is impressive: Emperor Charles V and Catherine de' Medici admired the work; Oliver Cromwell procured a manuscript copy, and adapted its principles to the Commonwealth government in England; Henry III and Henry IV of France were carrying copies when they were murdered; it helped Frederick the Great to shape Prussian policy; Louis XIV used the book as his 'favorite nightcap'; an annotated copy was found in Napoleon Bonaparte's coach at Waterloo; Napoleon III's ideas on government were chiefly derived from it; and Bismarck was a devoted disciple. More recently, Adolf Hitler, according to his own word, kept *The Prince* by his bedside, where it served as a constant source of inspiration; and Benito Mussolini stated, 'I believe Machiavelli's *Prince* to be the statesman's supreme guide. His doctrine is alive today because in the course of four hundred years no deep changes have occurred in the minds of men or in the actions of nations.'" Robert B. Downs, *Books That Changed the World* (1956; New York: Signet, 2004), chap. 12. *The Prince* is a central text in the education of leaders today. One of Machiavelli's more recent scholars, the University of Chicago political theorist Leo Strauss, rightly observed that Machiavelli was a teacher of evil and that gaining and maintaining power is not about ethics, as so many assert. Leo Strauss, *Thoughts on Machiavelli* (Chicago: University of Chicago Press, 1995).

19 **time of extreme violence:** Steven Pinker, *The Better Angels of Our Nature: Why Violence Has Declined* (New York: Viking, 2011).

20 **"force and fraud":** For an excellent biography of Machiavelli, see Ross King, *Machiavelli: Philosopher of Power* (New York: HarperPerennial, 2007). For an excellent historical treatment of his thinking about power, see Harvey C. Mansfield, *Machiavelli's Virtue* (Chicago: University of Chicago Press, 1966).

20 **world without coercive force:** For an exhilarating tour of such historical examples, see Howard Zinn, *A Power Governments Cannot Suppress* (San Francisco: City Lights, 2007).

20 **examined 323 opposition movements:** E. Chenowith and M. J. Stephan, "Why Civil Resistance Works: The Strategic Logic of Nonviolent Conflict," *International Security* 33, no. 1 (2008).

21 **less power and influence:** Cameron Anderson, Oliver P. John, and Dacher Keltner, "The Personal Sense of Power: An Interactionist Approach," *Journal of Personality* 80 (2012): 313–44.

21 **abusing their children:** D. B. Bugental and J. C. Lewis, "The Paradoxical Misuse of Power by Those Who See Themselves as Powerless: How Does It Happen?" *Journal of Social Issues* 55 (1999): 51–64.

21 **rank near the bottom:** Most studies find that of the 15 percent or so of any grammar school sample that is identified as bullies, about 10 percent are popular, and the rest are not popular or are actively rejected by their peers. See M. J. Boulton and P. K. Smith, "Bully/Victim Problems in Middle-School Children: Stability, Self-Perceived Competence, Peer Perceptions, and Peer Acceptance," *British Journal of Developmental Psychology* 12 (1994): 315–29.

22 **"the fundamental concept":** Bertrand Russell, *Power: A New Social Analysis* (London: Allen and Unwin, 1938), 10.

22 **warmth and understanding:** Anne Koenig, Alice Eagly, Abigail Mitchell, and Tiina Ristikari, "Are Leader Stereotypes Masculine: A Meta-Analysis of Three Research Programs," *Psychological Bulletin* 137, no. 4 (2011): 616–42. In this important paper, Koenig and her colleagues synthesized nearly forty years of studies that captured people's beliefs about what it takes to gain power. The studies' participants came from Western, East Asian, and Middle Eastern cultures.

23 **difference in the world:** Steven Lukes, ed., *Power: A Radical View* (New York: New York University Press, 1986).

23 **only 10 to 15 percent:** Cameron Anderson, Oliver P. John, and Dacher Keltner, "The Personal Sense of Power: An Interactionist Approach," *Journal of Personality* 80 (2012): 313–44.

25 **led to the end of slavery:** Adam Hochschild, *Bury the Chains: Prophets and Rebels in the Fight to Free an Empire's Slaves* (New York: Houghton Mifflin, 2004).

26 **real, true, and fair:** Harvard scholar Joseph Nye has called this power of cultural ideas, values, and practices "soft power" and made the argument, in *The Future of Power*, that a nation's soft power is as consequential as its "hard power"—military actions like drone strikes, waterboarding, or boots on the ground.

27 **Victorian-era tea set:** For more on this theme, it's worth listening to the BBC's *History of the World in 100 Objects*, which tells the history of humankind in one hundred objects, giving fifteen-minute riffs on some of our species' most influential creations: a 1.5-million-year-old hand ax from Olduvai Gorge, an Olmec stone mask, a pot from China, a flood tablet, and a credit card. And across these hundred objects, power is one of the most common themes.

27 **imbues every manufactured object:** For a wonderful tour of the signs of social class, see Paul Fussell, *Class: A Guide Through the American Status System* (New York: Touchstone, 1983).

29 **is part of every relationship:** A. P. Fiske, "Four Elementary Forms of Sociality: Framework for a Unified Theory of Social Relations," *Psychological Review* 99 (1992): 689–723.

29 **competitively vying for nutrients:** D. Haig, "Genetic Conflicts in Human Pregnancy," *Quarterly Review of Biology* 68 (1993): 495–532.

30 **siblings develop identities:** Frank Sulloway, *Born to Rebel: Birth Order, Family Dynamics, and Revolutionary Genius* (New York: Pantheon, 1996).

30 **as professional baseball players:** Frank J. Sulloway and R. L. Zweigenhaft, "Birth Order and Risk Taking in Athletics: A Meta-Analysis and Study of Major League Baseball Players," *Personality and Social Psychology Review* 14 (2010): 402–16.

30 **mutually empowered couples:** T. Falbo and L. A. Peplau, "Power Strategies in

Intimate Relationships," *Journal of Personality and Social Psychology* 38, no. 4 (1981): 618–28.

31 woman feels disempowered: E. O. Laumann, A. Paik, and R. C. Rosen, "Sexual Dysfunction in the United States: Prevalence and Predictors," *JAMA* 281 (1999): 537–44.

31 not named as often as friends: D. B. Hecht, H. M. Inderbirtzen, and A. L. Bukowski, "The Relationship Between Peer Status and Depressive Symptoms in Children and Adolescents," *Journal of Abnormal Child Psychology* 26 (1998): 153–60.

33 How people parent: D. Baumrind, "Child Care Practices Anteceding Three Patterns of Preschool Behavior," *Genetic Psychology Monographs* 75, no. 1 (1967): 43–88.

34 instantaneously when humans interact: For a review of this scholarship, see Cameron Anderson and G. Kilduff, "The Pursuit of Status in Social Groups," *Current Directions in Psychological Science* 18 (2009): 295–98.

34 summer camp life: R. C. Savin-Williams, "Dominance in a Human Adolescent Group," *Animal Behavior* 25 (1977): 400–6.

34 go to kindergarten: Dacher Keltner, Deborah Gruenfeld, and Cameron Anderson, "Power, Approach, and Inhibition," *Psychological Review* 110, no. 2 (2003): 265–84.

34 speaking up first: Cameron Anderson and G. Kilduff, "Why Do Dominant Personalities Attain Influence in Groups? A Competence-Signaling Account of Personality Dominance," *Journal of Personality and Social Psychology* 96 (2009).

34 simple acts that bind: For a recent compilation of inspiring stories about people making a difference in the world through everyday acts, see Nicholas D. Kristof and Sheryl WuDunn, *A Path Appears: Transforming Lives, Creating Opportunity* (New York: Knopf, 2014).

35 always in flux: D. S. Moskowitz, "Cross-Situational Generality and the Interpersonal Circumplex," *Journal of Personality and Social Psychology* 66 (1994): 921–33.

35 negotiated nearly every hour: Frans de Waal, *Chimpanzee Politics* (Baltimore: Johns Hopkins University Press, 1982).

35 identify a single leader: Christopher Boehm, *Hierarchy in the Forest: The Evolution of Egalitarian Behavior* (Cambridge, MA: Harvard University Press, 1999).

36 working in teams: Greg L. Stewart, Charles C. Manz, and Henry P. Sims, Jr., *Team Work and Group Dynamics* (New York: Wiley, 1999).

36 number of authors: Stefan Wuchty, B. F. Jones, and B. Uzzi, "The Increasing Dominance of Teams in Production of Knowledge," *Science* 316 (2007): 1036–39.

37 "Power corresponds to": Hannah Arendt, *On Violence* (New York: Harcourt Brace, 1969), 44.

37 "employed and exercised": Michel Foucault, *Power/Knowledge: Selected Interviews and Other Writings, 1972–1976* (New York: Pantheon, 1976), 98.

38 typically collaboratively, moving: E. O. Wilson, *Social Conquest of Earth* (New York: Liveright, 2012).

39 catalysts of influence: James Fowler and Nicolas Christakis, *Connected: The Surprising Power of Our Social Networks* (New York: Little, Brown, 2009).

39 feels good, in a particular: Dacher Keltner, Deborah Gruenfeld, and Cameron Anderson, "Power, Approach, and Inhibition," *Psychological Review* 110, no. 2 (2003): 265–84.

Chapter 2: Power Is Given, Not Grabbed

41 **a place of bullying:** William Golding, *Lord of the Flies* (Boston: Faber & Faber, 1954).

43 **the greater good:** For an excellent discussion of the idea of the greater good, see Darrin McMahon, *Happiness: A History* (New York: Atlantic Monthly Press, 2005). McMahon deals with the historical origins of the concept and how utilitarian philosophers grappled with questions concerning it, such as: How many people are benefited? How does one scale the intensity of benefit or harm? And who defines harm and benefit in the first place?

46 **produce greater trust:** When individuals in groups orient toward enhancing others' welfare, as opposed to prioritizing their own to advance at the expense of others, typically those groups fare better. Robert Nowak and Eugene Highfield, *Super Cooperators: Altruism, Evolution, and Why We Need Each Other to Succeed* (New York: Free Press, 2011).

47 **their social rank says:** A. Öhman, "Face the Beast and Fear the Face: Animal and Social Fears as Prototypes for Evolutionary Analyses of Emotion," *Psychophysiology* 23 (1986): 123–45.

47 **one hall in a first-year dorm:** Cameron Anderson, Oliver P. John, Dacher Keltner, and Ann M. Kring, "Who Attains Social Status? Effects of Personality and Physical Attractiveness in Social Groups," *Journal of Personality and Social Psychology* 81 (2001): 116–32.

48 **the Big Five:** Oliver P. John, Laura P. Naumann, and Christopher J. Soto, "Paradigm Shift to the Integrative Big Five Trait Taxonomy: History, Measurement, and Conceptual Issues," in *Handbook of Personality: Theory and Research*, eds. Oliver P. John, Richard W. Robins, and Lawrence A. Pervin (New York: Guilford, 2008): 114–58.

48 **advance the greater good:** In the terminology of this science, enthusiasm is referred to as "extraversion," kindness as "agreeableness," and focus as "conscientiousness." Calm actually is reversed semantically and known as "neuroticism," while openness goes by the name "openness to experience." Studies from many different countries find that these five tendencies organize how people perceive other individuals and themselves.

49 **limited in profound ways:** One of the most critical issues in social psychology is that so many studies limit their samples to middle-class western European college students. Hence, for many claims in this book, confidence is bolstered when studies test hypotheses with different age groups, people from different class backgrounds, and people from non-Western cultures. For a forceful statement, see Joseph Henrich, Steven J. Heine, and Ara Norenzayan, "The Weirdest People in the World?," *Behavioral and Brain Sciences* 33 (2010): 61–83.

50 **those who rose to power:** T. A. Judge, J. E. Bono, R. Ilies, and M. W. Gerhardt, "Personality and Leadership: A Qualitative and Quantitative Review," *Journal of Applied Psychology* 87 (2002): 465–80. There are a few contextual variations in how the Big Five relate to power. Kindness is only weakly related to the rise in power in business contexts (but it doesn't cost people in business). And focus proves to be more important in military units.

50   **summary of forty-eight studies:** Christopher Boehm, "Egalitarian Behavior and Reverse Dominance Hierarchy," *Current Anthropology* 33 (1993): 227–54.

51   **observing a community of chimps:** Frans de Waal, *Chimpanzee Politics* (Baltimore: Johns Hopkins University Press, 1982); the quotation is at p. 145.

54   **Reputation is the judgment:** For a lucid discussion of distinctions between reputation and personality, and the "reputational discourse" processes in which collectives establish group members' reputations, see Kenneth H. Craik, *Reputation: A Network Interpretation* (New York: Oxford University Press, 2009).

55   **impressions of the character:** Our coding of the reputation narratives was guided by Jonathan Haidt's conceptualization of different moral domains. For the latest treatment of this science, see Haidt's *The Righteous Mind: Why Good People Are Divided by Politics and Religion* (New York: Pantheon, 2012).

55   **marking them with reputations:** This study is reported on in Dacher Keltner, Gerben A. Van Kleef, Serena Chen, and Michael W. Kraus, "A Reciprocal Influence Model of Social Power: Emerging Principles and Lines of Inquiry," in *Advances in Experimental Social Psychology*, ed. M. A. Zanna (London: Academic Press, 2008): 40:151–92.

55   **the bad apples:** W. Felps, T. Mitchell, and E. Byington, "How, When, and Why Bad Apples Spoil the Barrel: Negative Group Members and Dysfunctional Groups," *Review of Organizational Behavior* 27 (2006): 175–222.

57   **arrive quickly at intuitions:** In one study that makes this point, participants played a game in which they could give some money to a stranger depending on how trustworthy that person was. Before making their gift, participants watched the stranger in a twenty-second soundless video clip as he or she listened to another person off camera describe an experience of suffering. From genetic assays of the strangers, I had identified individuals according to whether their genetic profile was associated with higher levels of oxytocin, a chemical that enables people to reach out to others, to be kinder, more open to others' emotions, and calmer. Participants wisely gave more money to people who were likely to have higher oxytocin levels and act in ways that advanced the greater good. A. Kogan et al., "A Thin-Slicing Study of the Oxytocin Receptor (OXTR) Gene and the Evaluation and Expression of the Prosocial Disposition," *Proceedings for the National Academy of Sciences* 108 (2011): 19189–92.

57   **Such reputations persist:** R. S. Burt, M. Kilduff, and S. Tasselli, "Social Network Analysis: Foundations and Frontiers on Advantage," *Annual Review of Psychology* 64 (2013): 527–47.

57   **direct more resources to you:** For an excellent summary of the recent science of cooperation, see D. G. Rand and M. A. Nowak, "Human Cooperation," *Trends in Cognitive Sciences* 17 (2013): 413–25.

58   **even incidental exposure:** M. Rigdon, K. Ishii, M. Watabe, and S. Kitayama, "Minimal Social Cues in the Dictator Game," *Journal of Economic Psychology* 30 (2009): 358–67.

58   **participants' selfish tendency:** One of my favorite demonstrations of the power of sensing that others are looking at you and evaluating your reputation is this one. Melissa Bateson explored the effects of the feeling of being seen in the coffee room in her department of psychology at the University of Newcastle. Psychologists—her

colleagues in the department—were the unsuspecting participants. The distribution of coffee and the milk used to make it less bitter ran according to an honor system. People were free to kick in money for milk according to their whim and the change jingling in their pockets. When an image of flowers was placed on a wall near the coffee dispenser, people on average gave fifteen pence for every liter of milk. When an image of the stern face of a male faced them in the very same place, those same colleagues gave seventy pence. Melissa Bateson, D. Nettle, and G. Roberts, "Cues of Being Watched Enhance Cooperation in a Real-World Setting," *Biology Letters* 2 (2006): 412–14.

59 **twelve food-sharing partners:** Kent Flannery and Joyce Marcus, *The Creation of Inequality* (Cambridge, MA: Harvard University Press, 2012).

60 **ritualistically give away food:** For an imaginative series of essays on the underappreciated relationship between food and status, see Polly Wiessner and Wulf Schiefenhövel, eds., *Food and the Status Quest* (Providence, RI: Bergahn Books, 1996).

60 **in exchange for actions:** This trade is seen today in laboratory studies: participants rank the status of individuals who have acted generously higher than they rank those who have not. Social scientists have named this trade "competitive altruism," noting that the self-interested pursuit of status and esteem can generate arms races of altruism. For articles on these ideas, see C. Hardy and M. Van Vugt, "Nice Guys Finish First: The Competitive Altruism Hypothesis," *Personality and Social Psychology Bulletin* 32 (2006): 1402–13, and R. Willer, "Groups Reward Individual Sacrifice: The Status Solution to the Collective Action Problem," *American Sociological Review* 74 (2009): 23–43.

60 **we esteem individuals:** Robert M. Hauser and John Robert Warren, "Socioeconomic Indexes for Occupations: A Review, Update, and Critique," *Sociological Methodology* 27, no. 1 (1997): 177–298.

60 **status and power are separable:** For an excellent discussion of the distinctions between status and power, see Joe C. Magee and Adam D. Galinsky, "Social Hierarchy: The Self-Reinforcing Nature of Power and Status," *Academy of Management Annals* 2 (2008): 351–98, and Susan T. Fiske, "Interpersonal Stratification: Status, Power, and Subordination," in *Handbook of Social Psychology*, 5th ed., eds. S. T. Fiske, D. T. Gilbert, and G. Lindzey (New York: Wiley & Sons, 2010): 941–82.

60 **Wall Street financier:** One example of how the powerful can routinely be held in low esteem is the reliable finding that U.S. citizens hold Goldman Sachs, one of the most profitable companies in history, in low esteem. Kai Ryssdal, "Goldman Sachs' Reputation Sinks Even Lower," Marketplace.org, February 6, 2015, http://bit .ly/1EzrDYk.

61 **valued, empowered, and esteemed:** Dacher Keltner and Brenda N. Buswell, "Embarrassment: Its Distinct Form and Appeasement Functions," *Psychological Bulletin* 122 (1997): 250–70.

61 **outright praise and adoration:** Erving Goffman, "The Nature of Deference and Demeanor," *American Anthropologist* 58 (1956): 473–502.

61 **the tactics of politeness:** Penelope Brown and Steven J. Levinson, *Politeness: Some Universals in Language Usage* (Cambridge, UK: Cambridge University Press, 1987).

62   **status-elevating expressions:** T. K. Inagaki and N. Eisenberger, "Shared Neural
      Mechanisms Underlying Social and Physical Warmth," *Psychological Science* 24
      (2013): 2272–80.

62   **pursuit of status:** George Borgas and Kirk G. Doran, "Prizes and Productivity: How
      Winning the Fields Medal Affects Scientific Output," *Journal of Human Resources*
      (in press).

62   **arms races of generosity:** Today in economic studies of prosocial behavior, scien-
      tists have begun to chart how the pursuit of status motivates all manner of altruistic
      behaviors, from charity to volunteerism. P. Barclay, "Trustworthiness and 'Competi-
      tive Altruism' Can Also Solve the 'Tragedy of the Commons,'" *Evolution and Human
      Behavior* 25 (2004): 209–20.

63   **gossiping ranks among:** For excellent cultural histories of gossip and other reputa-
      tional discourse, see Roger Wilkes, *Scandal: A Scurrilous History of Gossip* (London:
      Atlantic Books, 2002), and John Whitfield, *People Will Talk: The Surprising Science of
      Reputation* (New York: John Wiley & Sons, 2012).

63   **keep the powerful in check:** Christopher Boehm, "Egalitarian Behavior and Re-
      verse Dominance Hierarchy," *Current Anthropology* 33 (1993): 227–54.

63   **of a person's character:** Joseph Epstein, *Gossip* (New York: Houghton Mifflin
      Harcourt, 2011).

64   **U.S. presidential campaigns:** Gail Collins, *Scorpion Tongues: Gossip, Celebrity, and
      American Politics* (New York: HarperPerennial, 1998).

64   **sorority sisters at UC Berkeley:** This study is reported on in Dacher Keltner, Gerben
      A. van Kleef, Serena Chen, and Michael W. Kraus, "A Reciprocal Influence Model of
      Social Power: Emerging Principles and Lines of Inquiry," in *Advances in Experimental
      Social Psychology*, ed. M. A. Zanna (London: Academic Press, 2008): 40:151–92.

65   **Gossip tarnishes the reputations:** For an early conceptual treatment of gossip in
      the social scientific literature, see R. I. M. Dunbar, "Gossip in Evolutionary Perspec-
      tive," *Review of General Psychology* 8 (2002): 100–10.

65   **a crew of strapping rowers:** K. M. Kniffin and D. S. Wilson, "Utilities of Gossip
      Across Organizational Levels," *Human Nature* 16 (2005): 278–92.

65   **keep their fences in order:** Robert Ellickson, *Order Without Law: How Neighbors
      Settle Disputes* (Cambridge, MA: Harvard University Press, 1994).

65   **we pass along every act:** R. Baumeister, L. Zhang, and K. Vohs, "Gossip as Cultural
      Learning," *Review of General Psychology* 8 (2004): 111–21.

66   **The first newspapers:** Roger Wilkes, *Scandal: A Scurrilous History of Gossip* (Lon-
      don: Atlantic Books, 2002).

66   **on websites and blogs:** Daniel J. Solove, *The Future of Reputation* (New Haven, CT:
      Yale University Press, 2007).

67   **in which participants could gossip:** M. Feinberg, R. Willer, and M. Schultze, "Gos-
      sip and Ostracism Promote Cooperation in Groups," *Psychological Science* 25, no. 3
      (2014): 656–64.

Chapter 3: Enduring Power Comes from a Focus on Others

69   **a sacred, living force:** Kent Flannery and Joyce Marcus, *The Creation of Inequality*
      (Cambridge, MA: Harvard University Press, 2012).

70   **social dynamics of friends:** C. A. Langner and Dacher Keltner, "Social Power and Emotional Experience: Actor and Partner Effects Within Dyadic Interactions," *Journal of Experimental Social Psychology* 44 (2008): 848–56; Cameron Anderson and Jennifer Berdahl, "The Experience of Power: Examining the Effects of Power on Approach and Inhibition Tendencies," *Journal of Personality and Social Psychology* 83 (2002): 1362–77.

70   **people at random times:** Cameron Anderson, Oliver P. John, and Dacher Keltner, "The Personal Sense of Power: An Interactionist Approach," *Journal of Personality* 80 (2012): 313–44.

70   **sharply attuned to rewards:** A. Guinote, "Power and Goal Pursuit," *Personality and Social Psychology Bulletin* 33 (2007): 1076–87.

70   **take risky gambles:** Cameron Anderson and Adam Galinsky, "Power, Optimism, and Risk-Taking," *European Journal of Social Psychology* 36 (2006): 511–36

74   **Lincoln's power is:** In one relevant study, a group of historians independently assessed each president's success and legacy and ranked Lincoln in the top four. Another group of historians rated each president in terms of his Big Five, which they arrived at through their in-depth study of letters, speeches, and biographies. Correlating these two sets of measures, we find that the U.S. presidents with great legacies in U.S. history tended to be oriented toward advancing the greater good (Principle 5): they were enthusiastic, tender and kind, focused, open to ideas and other people's feelings, and calm. Stephen J. Rubenzer and Thomas Faschingbauer, *Personality, Character, and Leadership in the White House: Psychologists Assess the Presidents* (Washington, DC: Brassey's, 2004).

74   **"His mind is at once":** Quoted in Doris Kearns Goodwin, *Team of Rivals* (New York: Simon & Schuster, 2012), p. 289.

74   **relate to one another:** Dacher Keltner and Ann M. Kring, "Emotion, Social Function, and Psychopathology," *Review of General Psychology* 2 (1998): 320–42.

74   **evoke specific reactions:** U. Dimberg and A. Ohman, "Behold the Wrath: Psychophysiological Responses to Facial Stimuli," *Motivation and Emotion* 20, no. 2 (1996): 149–82.

75   **Paying careful attention:** Marc A. Brackett, Susan E. Rivers, and Peter Salovey, "Emotional Intelligence: Implications for Personal, Social, Academic, and Workplace Success," *Social and Personality Psychology Compass* 5, no. 1 (2011): 88–103, and J. D. Mayer, S. G. Barsade, and R. D. Roberts, "Human Abilities: Emotional Intelligence," *Annual Review of Psychology* 59 (2008): 507–36.

76   **perspective and poise:** M. D. Lieberman et al., "Putting Feelings Into Words: Affect Labeling Disrupts Amygdala Activity in Response to Affective Stimuli," *Psychological Science* 18, no. 5 (2007): 421–28.

76   **practical intelligence tasks:** Anita W. Woolley et al., "Evidence for a Collective Intelligence Factor in the Performance of Human Groups," *Science*, September 30, 2010, doi:10.1126/science.1193147.

76   **Having more women:** "The CS Gender 3000: Women in Senior Management," Credit Suisse, September 2014.

82   **Empathy tests measure:** J. D. Mayer and Peter Salovey, "The Intelligence of Emotional Intelligence," *Intelligence* 17, no. 4 (1993): 433–42.

82   **a sharp focus on other people's emotions:** For a summary of the benefits of high emotional intelligence, see Marc A. Brackett, Susan E. Rivers, and Peter Salovey, "Emotional Intelligence: Implications for Personal, Social, Academic, and Workplace Success," *Social and Personality Psychology Compass* 5, no. 1 (2011): 88–103, and J. D. Mayer, S. G. Barsade, and R. D. Roberts, "Human Abilities: Emotional Intelligence," *Annual Review of Psychology* 59 (2008): 507–36.

82   **do better work:** Stéphane Côté and C. T. H. Miners, "Emotional Intelligence, Cognitive Intelligence, and Job Performance," *Administrative Science Quarterly* 51 (2012): 1–28.

82   **led by empathetic managers:** For an excellent review of the recent literature on emotional intelligence in the workplace, see Stéphane Côté, "Emotional Intelligence in Organizations," *Review of Organizational Psychology* 1 (2014): 459–88.

83   **essential to achieving enduring power:** Here are a few more science-based tips for cultivating empathy. We can sharpen our focus on others by learning a bit about facial expression and vocalization and touch—how we communicate emotion. Asking open-ended questions and listening in a nonjudgmental fashion are critical. When parents take the time to ask about their children's emotions in nonjudgmental ways, in particular in the heat of a confrontation or sibling conflict, the empathy scores of their children rise. Judy Dunn, "The Development of Individual Differences in Understanding Emotion and Mind: Antecedents and Sequelae," in *Feelings and Emotions: The Amsterdam Symposium*, eds. Nico H. Frijda, Antony S. R. Manstead, and Agneta Fischer (New York: Cambridge University Press, 2004). Reading fiction enhances empathy as well. K. Oatley, J. B. Peterson, "Exploring the Link Between Reading Fiction and Empathy: Ruling Out Individual Differences and Examining Outcomes," *Communications: The European Journal of Communication* 34 (2009): 407–28.

83   **touch is a powerful:** For a review of the science of touch, see Dacher Keltner, *Born to Be Good: The Science of a Meaningful Life* (New York: W. W. Norton, 2009).

83   **release of oxytocin:** Kerstin Uvnäs Morberg, *The Oxytocin Factor* (Cambridge, UK: Cambridge University Press, 2003).

83   **the orbitofrontal cortex:** Edmund Rolls, *Emotions Explained* (Oxford: Oxford University Press, 2005).

84   **touches of appreciation:** For a review see Keltner, *Born to Be Good*, chap. 9.

84   **neurophysiology of stress:** D. Francis and M. J. Meaney, "Maternal Care and the Development of Stress Responses," *Development* 9 (1999): 28–34.

84   **holding the hand:** J. A. Coan, H. S. Schaefer, and R. J. Davidson, "Lending a Hand: Social Regulation of the Neural Response to Threat," *Psychological Science* 17 (2006): 1032–39.

84   **cried less when:** Larry Gray, Lisa Watt, and Elliott M. Blass, "Skin-to-Skin Contact Is Analgesic in Healthy Newborns," *Pediatrics* 105 (2000): 14–20.

84   **touch would empower others:** Michael W. Kraus, C. Huang, and Dacher Keltner, "Tactile Communication, Cooperation, and Performance: An Ethological Study of the NBA," *Emotion* 10 (2010): 745–49.

86   **"the essence of being human":** Desmond Tutu, *No Future Without Forgiveness* (New York: Doubleday, 1999).

87 **"The duties of gratitude":** Adam Smith, *The Theory of Moral Sentiments* (1759).

87 **the reverence we feel:** For an excellent overview of the science of gratitude, see Robert A. Emmons, *Thanks: How the New Science of Gratitude Can Make You Happier* (New York: Houghton Mifflin, 2007).

88 **the grateful mindset:** R. A. Emmons and Michael McCullough, "Counting Blessings Versus Burdens: An Experimental Investigation of Gratitude and Subjective Well-Being in Daily Life," *Journal of Personality and Social Psychology* 84, no. 2 (2003): 377–89.

88 **Chimpanzees share food:** Frans de Waal, "The Chimpanzees Service Economy: Food for Sharing," *Evolution and Human Behavior* 18 (1997): 375–86.

88 **a large barrier:** Matthew J. Hertenstein, Rachel Holmes, Margaret McCullough, and Dacher Keltner, "The Communication of Emotion via Touch," *Emotion* 9 (2009): 566–73.

89 **have stronger ties:** S. B. Algoe, Jonathan Haidt, and Shelly L. Gable, "Beyond Reciprocity: Gratitude and Relationships in Everyday Life," *Emotion* 8 (2008): 425–29.

89 **Teachers who cultivate:** Robert A. Emmons, *Thanks: How the New Science of Gratitude Can Make You Happier* (New York: Houghton Mifflin, 2007).

89 **partners who subtly expressed:** A. M. Gordon et al., "To Have and to Hold: Gratitude Promotes Relationship Maintenance in Intimate Bonds," *Journal of Personality and Social Psychology* 103 (2012): 257–74.

90 **cooperate with a stranger:** F. N. Willis and H. K. Hamm, "The Use of Interpersonal Touch in Securing Compliance," *Journal of Nonverbal Behavior* 5, no. 1 (1980): 49–55; R. Kurzban, "The Social Psychophysics of Cooperation: Nonverbal Communication in a Public Goods Game," *Journal of Nonverbal Behavior* 25 (2001): 241–59.

90 **grateful pats to the back:** N. Gueguen, "Nonverbal Encouragement of Participation in a Course: The Effect of Touching," *Social Psychology of Education* 7 (2004): 89–98.

90 **helped the experimenter:** A. Grant and F. Gino, "A Little Thanks Goes a Long Way: Explaining Why Gratitude Expressions Motivate Prosocial Behavior," *Journal of Personality and Social Psychology* 98, no. 6 (2010): 946–55.

90 **when it crashed:** M. Y. Bartlett and D. DeSteno, "Gratitude and Prosocial Behavior: Helping When It Costs You," *Psychological Science* 17 (2006): 319–25.

92 **an entire fraternity:** Dacher Keltner et al., "Teasing in Hierarchical and Intimate Relations," *Journal of Personality and Social Psychology* 75 (1998): 1231–47.

93 **a summer basketball camp:** Michael W. Kraus et al., "Taunting, Teasing, and the Politics of Politeness: How Sociometric Status Gives Rise to Expectation-Consistent Action," *PLoS ONE* 9, no. 8 (2014): e104737.

95 **good amounts of teasing:** For a review of work on the benefits and perils of teasing, see Dacher Keltner et al., "Just Teasing: A Conceptual Analysis and Empirical Review," *Psychological Bulletin* 127 (2001): 229–48.

95 **stories are a powerful tool:** James Pennebaker, *Writing to Heal: A Guided Journal for Recovery from Trauma and Emotional Upheaval* (Oakland, CA: New Harbinger, 2004).

95 **Our identity and purpose:** D. P. McAdams, "The Psychology of Life Stories," *Review of General Psychology* 5 (2001): 100–22.

Chapter 4: The Abuses of Power

100 constrain the powerful: For a general discussion of processes that keep the powerful in check, see Dacher Keltner, Deborah Gruenfeld, and Cameron Anderson, "Power, Approach and Inhibition," *Psychological Review* 110, no. 2 (2003): 265–84. In one study participants who were made to feel powerful made more self-serving and riskier decisions with other people's money, except when they knew they would be accountable for their decisions and would have to justify them to others. M. Pitesa and S. Thau, "Masters of the Universe: How Power and Accountability Influence Self-Serving Decisions Under Moral Hazard," *Journal of Applied Psychology* 98 (2013): 550–58.

101 less dependent upon others: S. L. Neuberg and S. T. Fiske, "Motivational Influences on Impression Formation: Outcome Dependency, Accuracy-Driven Attention, and Individuating Processes," *Journal of Personality and Social Psychology* 53 (1987): 431–44.

104 momentary shifts in power: Michael W. Kraus, Stéphane Côté, and Dacher Keltner, "Social Class, Contextualism, and Empathic Accuracy," *Psychological Science* 21 (2010): 1716–23.

106 capacity to mimic others: S. D. Preston and Frans de Waal, "Empathy: Its Ultimate and Proximate Bases," *Behavioral and Brain Sciences* 25 (2002): 1–71.

106 an instinct for mimicry: For examples of mimicry, see U. Dimberg, M. Thunberg, and S. Grunedal, "Facial Reactions to Emotional Stimuli: Automatically Controlled Emotional Responses," *Cognition and Emotion* 16 (2002): 449–71, and R. S. Miller, "Empathic Embarrassment: Situational and Personal Determinants of Reactions to the Embarrassment of Another," *Journal of Personality and Social Psychology* 53 (1987): 1061–69.

108 a time when they felt powerful: J. Hogeveen, M. Inzlicht, and S. S. Obhi, "Power Changes the Way the Brain Responds to Others," *Journal of Experimental Psychology: General* (in press).

108 Mimicking others' nonverbal behaviors: J. L. Lakin, V. E. Jefferis, C. M. Cheng, and T. L. Chartrand, "The Chameleon Effect as Social Glue: Evidence for the Evolutionary Significance of Nonconscious Mimicry," *Journal of Nonverbal Behavior* 27 (2003): 145–62.

109 the empathy network of neurons in the brain's cortex: The specific brain regions that are considered part of the empathy or "mentalizing" network include the dorsomedial prefrontal cortex (DMPFC), the medial prefrontal cortex (MPFC), the precuneus/posterior cingulate cortex (PCC), the temporoparietal junction (TPJ), and the posterior superior temporal sulcus (pSTS).

109 an upper-class background: K. A. Muscatell et al., "Social Status Modulates Neural Activity in the Mentalizing Network," *Neuroimage* 60 (2012): 1771–77.

109 capacity to flexibly move: These ideas are found in literature on "integrative complexity," the process in which an individual takes multiple perspectives upon an issue or problem, be it a matter being negotiated, a conflict with an ideological adversary, or a problem in need of a solution. Integrative complexity produces better outcomes in social interactions like negotiations and brainstorming. See P. Suedfeld and P. Tetlock, "Integrative Complexity of Communications in International Crises," *Jour-*

nal of Conflict Resolution 21 (1977): 169–84; and Deborah Gruenfeld, "Status, Ideology, and Integrative Complexity on the U.S. Supreme Court: Rethinking the Politics of Political Decision Making," *Journal of Personality and Social Psychology* 68 (1995): 5–20.

110 **People feeling powerless:** Adam Galinsky, J. C. Magee, M. E. Inesi, and Deborah H. Gruenfeld, "Power and Perspectives Not Taken," *Psychological Science* 17 (2006): 1068–74.

111 **focused first on social class:** J. E. Stellar, V. M. Manzo, Michael W. Kraus, and Dacher Keltner, "Class and Compassion: Socioeconomic Factors Predict Responses to Suffering," *Emotion* 12 (2012): 449–59.

112 **poor individuals will be feeling:** Some may assume that the wealthy differ in some genetic way that brings about their lack of compassion, that they are born sociopaths or coldhearted. But evidence argues definitively against this conclusion. In our lab we have found a gene that relates to increased oxytocin in the nervous system, a chemical that leads to increased caring, empathy, and generosity. One tempting hypothesis would be that the rich and powerful lack this gene, that they have a biological temperament that predisposes them to compassion deficits. But in our research we never find class differences in who has or does not have this oxytocin-related gene. Instead, it is wiser to conclude that the possession of wealth, and being brought up in a life of privilege and power, diminishes our compassionate tendencies. See S. M. Rodrigues et al., "An Oxytocin Receptor Genetic Variation Relates to Empathy and Stress Reactivity in Humans," *Proceedings of the National Academy of Sciences* 106 (2009): 21437–41.

113 **activation in the vagus nerve:** S. Porges, "Love: An Emergent Property of the Mammalian Autonomic Nervous System," *Psychoendocrinology* 23 (1998): 837–61.

113 **increased sharing, cooperation:** Dacher Keltner, A. Kogan, Paul Piff, and S. Saturn, "The Sociocultural Appraisal, Values, and Emotions (SAVE) Model of Prosociality: Core Processes from Gene to Meme," *Annual Review of Psychology* 65 (2014): 425–60.

113 **a state of elevation:** S. Schnall, J. Roper, and D. M. T. Fessler, "Elevation Leads to Altruistic Behavior," *Psychological Science* 21 (2010): 315–20.

115 **vital to strong social networks:** Dacher Keltner and Jonathan Haidt, "Approaching Awe, a Moral, Aesthetic, and Spiritual Emotion," *Cognition and Emotion* 17 (2003): 297–314.

115 **inspired more by telling:** Gerben A. Van Kleef et al., "Power Gets You High: The Powerful Are More Inspired by Themselves Than by Others," *Social Psychological and Personality Science* (2015): 1–9.

116 **corrupting influence of power:** Dacher Keltner and J. Lerner, "Emotion," in *The Handbook of Social Psychology*, eds. S. Fiske and D. Gilbert (New York: McGraw-Hill, 2010).

116 **the dynamic relation:** J. Beer et al., "The Regulatory Function of Self-Conscious Emotion: Insights from Patients with Orbitofrontal Damage," *Journal of Personality and Social Psychology* 85, no. 5 (2003): 594–604.

116 **garden-variety sociopaths:** James Blair, Derek Mitchell, and Karina Blair, *The Psychopath: Emotion and the Brain* (Malden, MA: Blackwell, 2005).

117 **power influences how we eat:** This study is reported in Dacher Keltner, Deborah Gruenfeld, and Cameron Anderson, "Power, Approach and Inhibition," *Psychological Review* 110 (2003): 265–84.

119 **express sexual impulses:** J. S. Santelli, R. Lowry, N. Brener, and L. Robin, "The Association of Sexual Behaviors with Socioeconomic Status, Family Structure, and Race/Ethnicity Among U.S. Adolescents," *American Journal of Public Health* 90 (2000): 1582–88.

120 **cheated on their spouses:** J. Lammers et al., "Power Increases Infidelity Among Men and Women," *Psychological Science* 22 (2011): 1191–97.

120 **endorsements of unethical actions:** J. Lammers, D. A. Stapel, and Adam Galinsky, "Power Increases Hypocrisy: Moralizing in Reasoning, Immorality in Behavior," *Psychological Science* 21 (2010): 737–34.

121 **four-way stop in Berkeley:** Paul K. Piff et al., "Higher Social Class Predicts Increased Unethical Behavior," *Proceedings of the National Academy of Sciences* 109 (2012): 4086–91.

121 **listed the Mercedes:** You may wonder whether people's social class correlates with the value of their car. In other analyses, we examined that issue and found that a person's family wealth does correlate strongly with the Blue Book value of his or her car.

127 **profile of a shoplifter:** C. Blanco et al., "Prevalence and Correlates of Shoplifting in the United States: Results from the National Epidemiological Survey on Alcohol and Related Conditions (NESARC)," *American Journal of Psychiatry* 165 (2008): 905–13.

127 **Wealthier participants were more likely:** Long Wang and J. Keith Murnighan, "Money, Emotions, and Ethics Across Individuals and Countries," *Journal of Business Ethics* 125, no. 1 (2014): 163–76.

128 **laws of cooperative communication:** J. A. Hall, E. J. Coats, and L. S. LeBeau, "Non-verbal Behavior and the Vertical Dimension of Social Relations: A Meta-Analysis," *Psychological Bulletin* 131, no. 6 (2005): 898–924.

129 **such rules of kind speech:** For a brilliant and influential statement on how power influences the linguistic practices that make speech more polite in different cultures, see Penelope Brown and Stephen Levinson, *Politeness: Some Universals in Language Usage* (New York: Cambridge University Press, 2007).

129 **flat-out rudeness:** Christine Porath and Christine Pearson, "The Price of Incivility: Lack of Respect in the Workplace Hurts Morale—And the Bottom Line," *Harvard Business Review* (January–February 2013), and Christine Pearson and Christine Porath, *The Cost of Bad Behavior: How Incivility Damages Your Business and What to Do About It* (New York: Portfolio Penguin, 2009).

130 **people will blame victims:** Melvin J. Lerner, *The Belief in a Just World: A Fundamental Decision* (New York: Plenum Press, 1980).

130 **work at, on average, 1.2 jobs:** R. Costa-Lopes, J. F. Dovidio, C. R. Pereira, and J. T. Jost, "Social Psychological Perspectives on the Legitimation of Social Inequality: Past, Present, and Future," *European Journal of Social Psychology* 43 (2013): 229–37. For an excellent journalistic summary of stereotypes of the poor and how often they misrepresent the reality of the lives of the poor, such as how hard they work, see the following by Valerie Strauss: https://www.washingtonpost.com/blogs/answer-sheet/wp/2013/10/28/five-stereotypes-about-poor-families-and-education.

131 Our power blinds us: J. Lammers, D. A. Stapel, and Adam Galinsky, "Power Increases Hypocrisy: Moralizing in Reasoning, Immorality in Behavior," *Psychological Science* 21 (2010): 737–34.

131 the income gap: Jacob Hacker and Paul Pierson, *Winner-Take-All Politics: How Washington Made the Rich Richer and Turned Its Back on the Middle Class* (New York: Simon & Schuster, 2010).

132 average U.S. family incomes: Michael W. Kraus, Paul K. Piff, and Dacher Keltner, "Social Class, Sense of Control, and Social Explanation," *Journal of Personality and Social Psychology* 97 (2009): 992–1004. The graph was from Kevin Phillips, *Wealth and Democracy: A Political History of the American Rich* (New York: Broadway Books, 2002). Phillips was a speechwriter for President Nixon and an architect of the Southern Strategy—the Republican approach of campaigning in the language of fear, crime, and soft forms of racism. Later, though, Phillips became a leading critic of the rise of inequality in the United States, arguing that those with exceptional wealth have privileged access to political power and champion policies that guarantee that wealth.

133 survival-of-the-fittest theorizing: Carl Degler, *In Search of Human Nature: The Decline and Revival of Social Darwinism in American Social Thought* (New York: Oxford University Press, 1991).

133 Narratives of exceptionalism: Michael W. Kraus and Dacher Keltner, "Social Class Rank, Essentialism, and Punitive Judgment," *Journal of Personality and Social Psychology* 105 (2013): 247–61.

134 advocate harsher punishment: Ibid.

134 the official poverty level: Michael W. Kraus and B. Callaghan, "Noblesse Oblige? Social Status and Economic Inequality Maintenance Among Politicians," *PLoS ONE* 9, no. 1 (2014): e85293.

134 enter into academic disciplines: S. Leslie, A. Cimpian, M. Meyer, and E. Freeland, "Expectations of Brilliance Underlie Gender Distributions in Academic Disciplines," *Science* 347 (2015): 262–65.

135 effects of CEO behavior: J. Surowiecki, "Why CEO Reform Failed," *New Yorker*, April 20, 2015. See also Michael Dorff, *Indispensable and Other Myths: Why the CEO Pay Experiment Failed and How to Fix It* (Berkeley: University of California Press, 2014).

136 flirt even more: J. Kunstman and J. K. Maner, "Sexual Overperception: Power, Mating Goals, and Biases in Social Judgment," *Journal of Personality and Social Psychology* 100 (2011): 282–94.

136 focusing on the signs: Paul K. Piff et al., "Having Less, Giving More: The Influence of Social Class on Prosocial Behavior," *Journal of Personality and Social Psychology* 99 (2010): 771–84

Chapter 5: The Price of Powerlessness

137 costs of powerlessness: In this chapter I will use the words *powerless* and *powerlessness* in referring to people who live in poverty and in low-income neighborhoods, and whose social identities have been devalued and disempowered by history. I do so simply for purposes of simplicity and exposition, recognizing that such people can feel a great deal of power through the day, that they routinely make large differences in the world, and that the power they have lost through economics or history is not absolute but a matter of degree.

140 **a galvanizing discovery:** Nancy E. Adler et al.,"Socioeconomic Status and Health: The Challenge of the Gradient," *American Psychologist* 49 (1994): 15–24. A fuller review of Adler's work on social class and health is worthwhile, for what I report on here is just a thin slice of two and a half decades of important work, linking a lower-class background and poverty to every possible problematic health outcome. For a recent review, see Jenna Nobles, Miranda R. Weintraub, and Nancy Adler, "Subjective Socioeconomic Status and Health: Relationships Reconsidered," *Social Science and Medicine* 82 (2013): 58–66.

141 **more likely to face threat:** Sally S. Dickerson and Margaret E. Kemeny, "Acute Stressors and Cortisol Responses: A Theoretical Integration and Synthesis of Laboratory Research," *Psychological Bulletin* 130 (2004): 355–91.

141 **the stress hormone cortisol:** Robert M. Sapolsky, "The Influence of Social Hierarchy on Primate Health," *Science* 308, no. 5722 (2005): 648–52.

143 **more threatening physical environments:** Marilee Coriell and Nancy Adler, "Social Ordering and Health," in Bruce S. McEwen and H. Maurice Goodman, eds., *Handbook of Physiology*, sec. 7, *The Endocrine System*, vol. 4, *Coping with the Environment: Neural and Endocrine Mechanisms* (New York: Oxford University Press, 2001).

143 **sleep disruption amplifies:** M. P. Walker, "The Role of Sleep in Cognition and Emotion," *New York Academy of Sciences* 1156 (2009): 168–97.

144 **harsher physical treatment:** Jack Glaser, *Suspect Race: Causes and Consequences of Racial Profiling* (New York: Oxford University Press, 2014), and Devah Pager, *Marked: Race, Crime, and Finding Work in an Era of Mass Incarceration* (Chicago: University of Chicago Press, 2007).

144 **longer sentences than whites:** Jason Marsh, "Can We Reduce Implicit Bias in Criminal Justice?," *Greater Good*, April 28, 2015, www.greatergood.berkeley.edu.

144 **judge their résumés:** D. Pager, F. G. Fryer, and J. Spenkuch, "Racial Disparities in Job Finding and Offered Wages," *Journal of Law and Economics* 56 (August 2013): 633–89.

144 **When seeking housing:** M. A. Turner et al., "Housing Discrimination Against Racial and Ethnic Minorities 2012," U.S. Department of Housing and Urban Development, June 11, 2013, http://bit.ly/1NKT9EZ.

144 **being in the numerical minority:** D. P. Green, D. Z. Strolovitch, and J. S. Wong, "Defended Neighborhoods, Integration, and Racially Motivated Crime," *American Journal of Sociology* 104 (1998): 372–403.

145 **victims of sexual violence:** Peggy Reeves Sanday, "The Socio-Cultural Context of Rape: A Cross-Cultural Study," *Journal of Social Issues* 37 (1981): 5–27.

145 **face sexual harassment:** Jennifer Berdahl, "Harassment Based on Sex: Protecting Social Status in the Context of Gender Hierarchy," *Academy of Management Review* 32 (2007): 641–58.

145 **when the powerful act out:** Christine Porath and Christine Pearson, "The Price of Incivility: Lack of Respect in the Workplace Hurts Morale—And the Bottom Line," *Harvard Business Review* (2013), and Christine Pearson and Christine Porath,

The Cost of Bad Behavior: How Incivility Damages Your Business and What You Can Do About It (New York: Portfolio Penguin, 2009).

145 **the targets of such actions:** C. A. Langner and Dacher Keltner, "Social Power and Emotional Experience: Actor and Partner Effects Within Dyadic Interactions," *Journal of Experimental Social Psychology* 44 (2008): 848–56.

145 **Poorer children express:** Michael W. Kraus et al., "Social Class, Solipsism, and Contextualism: How the Rich Are Different from the Poor," *Psychological Review* 119 (2012): 546–72.

145 **more likely to shoplift:** E. Chen and K. A. Matthews, "Cognitive Appraisal Biases: An Approach to Understanding the Relation Between Socioeconomic Status and Cardiovascular Reactivity in Children," *Annals of Behavioral Medicine* 23 (2001): 101–11.

146 **activation in the amygdala:** P. J. Gianaros et al., "Potential Neural Embedding of Parental Social Standing," *Social, Cognitive, and Affective Neuroscience* (February 2008), doi:10.1093/scan/nsn003.

146 **speak up less:** Adam Galinsky, Deborah Gruenfeld, and J. Magee, "From Power to Action," *Journal of Personality and Social Psychology* 85 (2003): 453–66. See also Cameron Anderson and Jennifer Berdahl, "The Experience of Power: Examining the Effects of Power on Approach and Inhibition Tendencies," *Journal of Personality and Social Psychology* 83 (2002): 1362–67.

148 **the HPA axis:** A must-read on stress is Robert Sapolsky's *Why Zebras Don't Get Ulcers*, 3rd ed. (New York: Holt, 2004). See also Sally S. Dickerson, T. L. Gruenewald, and Margaret E. Kemeny, "Physiological Effects of Social Threat: Implications for Health," in *Handbook of Social Neuroscience*, eds. J. Cacioppo and J. Decety (New York: Oxford University Press, 2011); and S. M. Rodrigues, J. E. LeDoux, and Robert Sapolsky, "The Influence of Stress Hormones on Fear Circuitry," *Annual Review of Neuroscience* 32 (2009): 289–313.

148 **the immune system:** Sally S. Dickerson et al., "Social-Evaluative Threat and Proinflammatory Cytokine Regulation: An Experimental Laboratory Investigation," *Psychological Science* 20 (2009): 1237–44.

149 **triggers of cortisol release:** Ibid. See also Sally S. Dickerson, T. L. Gruenewald, and Margaret E. Kemeny, "When the Social Self Is Threatened: Shame, Physiology, and Health," *Journal of Personality* 72 (2004): 1192–216.

149 **biology of defense:** See Neha A. John-Henderson, M. Rheinschmidt, R. Mendoza-Denton, and D. D. Francis, "Performance and Inflammation Outcomes Predicted by Different Facets of SES Under Stereotype Threat," *Social Psychological and Personality Science* (2013): 1–9; and Neha A. John-Henderson, E. G. Jacobs, R. Mendoza-Denton, and D. D. Francis, "Wealth, Health, and the Moderating Role of Implicit Social Class Bias," *Annals of Behavioral Medicine* 45 (2013): 173–79.

149 **their cortisol rose:** D. Eliezer, B. Major, and W. B. Mendes, "The Costs of Caring: Gender Identification Increases Threat Following Exposure to Sexism," *Journal of Experimental Social Psychology* 46 (2010): 159–65.

149 **elevated physiological arousal:** W. B. Mendes, B. Major, S. McCoy, and J. Blascovich, "How Attributional Ambiguity Shapes Physiological and Emotional Responses to Social Rejection and Acceptance," *Journal of Personality and Social Psychology* 94 (2008): 278–91.

149 **promotions, salaries, or budget decisions:** G. Sherman et al., "Leadership Is Associated with Lower Levels of Stress," *Proceedings of the National Academy of Sciences* 109, no. 44 (2012): 17903–7.

149 **a powerless posture:** D. R. Carney, A. J. C. Cuddy, and A. J. Yap, "Power Poses: Brief Nonverbal Displays Cause Neuroendocrine Change and Increase Risk Tolerance," *Psychological Science* 21 (2010): 1363–68.

151 **the amount of myelin:** S. Chetty et al., "Stress and Glucocorticoids Promote Oligodendrogenesis in the Adult Hippocampus," *Molecular Psychiatry* 19 (2014): 1275–83.

152 **excitement in the sexual organs:** For a review of what power and powerlessness does to sexual behavior across species, see L. Ellis, "Dominance and Reproductive Success Among Nonhuman Animals: A Cross-Species Comparison," *Ethology and Sociobiology* 16 (1995): 257–333.

152 **to sexual dysfunction:** E. O. Laumann, A. Paik, and R. C. Rosen, "Sexual Dysfunction in the United States: Prevalence and Predictors," *JAMA* 281 (1999): 537–44.

152 **an experimenter lashed out:** Christine Porath and Christine Pearson, "The Cost of Bad Behavior," *Organizational Dynamics* 39, no. 1 (2010): 64–71.

153 **more than a thousand children:** K. G. Noble et al., "Family Income, Parental Education and Brain Development in Children and Adolescents," *Nature Neuroscience* 18 (2015): 773–78.

153 **are less happy than those:** Daniel Kahneman and Angus Deaton, "High Income Improves Evaluation of Life But Not Emotional Well-Being," *Proceedings of the National Academy of Sciences* 107, no. 38 (2010): 16489–93.

153 **to clinical anxiety:** Linda C. Gallo and Karen Matthews, "Understanding the Association Between Socioeconomic Status and Health: Do Negative Emotions Play a Role?," *Psychological Bulletin* 129 (2003): 10–51.

154 **major episodes of depression:** V. Lorant et al., "Socioeconomic Inequalities in Depression: A Meta-Analysis," *American Journal of Epidemiology* 157 (2002): 98–112.

154 **women's health over several months:** Nancy Adler, E. S. Epel, G. Castellazzo, and J. R. Ickovics, "Relationship of Subjective and Objective Social Status with Psychological and Physiological Functioning: Preliminary Data in Healthy, White Women," *Health Psychology* 19 (2000): 586–92.

155 **actually damages telomeres:** T. Robertson et al., "Is Socioeconomic Status Associated with Biological Aging as Measured by Telomere Length?" *Epidemiological Review* 35 (2013): 98–111.

155 **toxic for young children:** For an excellent review, see G. E. Miller, E. Chen, and K. Parker, "Psychological Stress in Childhood and Susceptibility to the Chronic Diseases of Aging: Moving Toward a Model of Behavioral and Biological Mechanisms," *Psychological Bulletin* 137 (2011): 959–97.

156 **chronically high levels:** G. E. Miller et al., "Low Early-Life Social Class Leaves a Biological Residue Manifested by Decreased Glucocorticoid and Increased Proinflammatory Signaling," *Proceedings of the National Academy of Sciences* 106, no. 34 (2009): 14716–21.

156 **greater cardiovascular response:** Ibid.

158 **When green spaces:** A lot of the evidence related to these and other approaches to improving the lives of people living in poverty is covered in a textbook I'm a coauthor

on: Tom Gilovich, Dacher Keltner, Serena Chen, and Richard Nisbett, *Social Psychology*, 4th ed. (New York: W. W. Norton, 2013).

Epilogue: A Fivefold Path to Power

161 **enjoy more enduring power:** Cameron Anderson, D. R. Ames, and S. D. Gosling, "The Perils of Status Self-Enhancement in Teams and Organizations," *Personality and Social Psychology Bulletin* 34 (2008): 90–101.

162 **the most important foundation:** L. B. Aknin et al., "Prosocial Spending and Well-Being: Cross-Cultural Evidence for a Psychological Universal," *Journal of Personality and Social Psychology* 104, no. 4 (2013): 635–52.

164 **desire for equality:** J. Henrich, R. Boyd, S. Bowles, and C. Camerer, "In Search of Homo Economicus: Behavioral Experiments in 15 Small-Scale Societies," *American Economic Review* 91, no. 2 (2001); D. G. Rand, J. D. Greene, and M. A. Nowak, "Spontaneous Giving and Calculated Greed," *Nature* 489, no. 7416 (2012): 427–30.

Index

abuses of power, 6–7, 8–9, 99–136
  absolute power, corrupting
    influence of, 99–101
  empathy deficits and diminished
    moral sentiments and, 101,
    103–16
  exceptionalism narratives and,
    101, 102–3, 130–35
  experience of power and, 69–70
  impulsivity and, 101, 102, 116–28
  incivility and disrespect and, 101,
    102, 128–30
  loss of focus and, 96–97, 101–2,
    103–16
acquired sociopathy, 116–17
Acton, John Dalberg-, Lord, 99, 116
advance greater good, power is given
    to those who, 5, 43, 44, 47–54
  calmness and, 49, 50
  enthusiasm and, 49, 50
  focus and, 49, 50
  in hunter-gatherer societies, 50–51
  kindness and, 49, 50
  openness and, 49, 50
  in primate social life, 51–54
  rise to power in dorm experiment,
    47–49
altruism, 62, 113–15

anxiety, 153
Apgar, Virginia, 25–26
Apgar score, 25–26
Aquinas, Thomas, 41–42
Arendt, Hannah, 36–37, 38, 50
Austen, Jane, 102
awards, 62
awareness of feelings of power, 160

back channel responses, 129
basketball performance, effect
    of touching on, 84–86
Beck, Glenn, 27
behaviors, and elevation of status,
    61–62
beliefs, altering, 26–27
Bentham, Jeremy, 44
Big Five concept, 50
biological explanations, for social
    hierarchies, 134–35
Black Lives Matter, 10
Bono, 27
British aristocracy, 132–33
Brown, Michael, 10

calmness, 49, 50
Campos, Memo, 138, 141
Campos, Willie, 138

Campos, Yolanda, 138
CEO compensation, 135
children
    brain development in, and chronic
        powerlessness, 152–53
    everday actions, power in, 34
    parent-child relationships, power
        in, 31–33
    poor health in, and social class,
        155–56
    storytelling and, 93–94
    threats, hypersensitivity to,
        145–46
Chimpanzee Politics (de Waal), 51
chimpanzees. *See* primates
Clarkson, Thomas, 25, 45
coercive force, and power, 2–3, 19–22
    Arendt on, 37
    Machiavelli on, 2, 19–20
Colbert, Stephen, 27
collaboration
    empathy and, 76
    empowering others in social
        networks and, 36
compassion, 86, 87, 101–2, 110
context-specific nature of power, 35
contribution to society,
        powerlessness impacting ability
        to contribute to. *See* society,
        powerlessness as impacting
        ability to contribute to
control, defined, 11
conversations, and empathy, 82–83
cooperative communication, 128–29
cortisol, 10, 141, 142, 148–51,
        155–56
cytokine system, 148–49, 155

daily acts of influence, 38–39
Darwin, Charles, 36, 87
Dear Abby, 26–27
depression, 154
de Waal, Frans, 51
difference in world, power as
        capacity to make, 3–4, 23–40

empowering others in social
        networks and, 23, 24, 36–39
everyday actions, power as element
        of, 23, 24, 33–35
relationships and interactions and,
        23, 24, 27–32
states of other people, altering, 23,
        24–27
disrespect. *See* incivility and
        disrespect
Downton Abbey (TV show), 102

eating, and impulsivity, 117–18
economic inequality, 9–10
    explanations of, 131–32
economic state, influencing, 24–25
Eichmann, Adolf, 37
elevation
    abuses of power and capacity for,
        101–2, 113–15
    through status and esteem
        (*See* esteem; status)
emotional expressions, 74–75
empathy, 8, 73–83
    abuse of power and deficits in,
        101–2, 103–16
    cartoons of emotional expressions,
        response to, 80–81
    collaborative interactions and, 76
    in conversations, 82–83
    costs associated with deficits in,
        110–11, 116
    defined, 103
    elevation, effect of feelings of
        power on, 113–15
    emotional expressions and,
        74–75
    experience of power as eroding
        capacity for, 106
    group performance on collective
        intelligence tests and impact of,
        76–80
    high-empathy individuals,
        performance of, 82
    increasing, methods for, 82–83

ladder exercise followed by test
for, results of, 104–6
listening and, 82
mimicry and, 106–8
open-ended questions and, 82
opinions of others, soliciting, 83
perspective taking, power as
undermining, 109–10
practicing, 75–76, 103–4
social class and capacity for,
108–9, 111–13
vagus nerve activation and, 113
empowering others in social
networks, 23, 24, 36–39
Arendt on, 37, 38
behavior's infectious nature
and, 39
collaboration and, 36
daily acts of influence and, 38–39
evolutionary roots of, 38
enthusiasm, 49, 50
esteem, 6, 43, 44, 59–63. *See also*
status
gratitude and, 89
touch and, 84
eugenics movement, 133
everyday actions, power as element
of, 23, 24, 33–35
context-specific nature of power
and, 35
emergence of power and, 34
leaderless group discussion
paradigm and, 33–34
simple actions and, 34–35
exceptionalism narratives, 101,
102–3, 130–35
academic disciplines with
prevailing, lack of low-power
group people entering, 134
blaming victims and, 130
of British aristocracy, 132–33
CEO compensation and, 135
effects of, 134–35
income gap, explanations of,
131–32

IQ testing and, 133
life events, 132–33
political decision making and, 134
rationalizing personal acts of
injustice and, 131
social hierarchies, biological
explanations for, 134–35
survival-of-the-fittest
theories, 133
experience of power
abuse of power and, 69–70
empathy, effect on capacity for, 106
focusing on others and, 69–71

Facebook, 14
fall from power, 6–7
fame, 23
Fascism, 22
Felker, Clay, 128
fight-or-flight behavior, 75, 148,
151–52
fivefold path to enduring power,
159–64
awareness of feelings of power, 160
generosity, practicing, 161–62
humility, practicing, 160–61
psychological context of
powerlessness, changing,
163–64
respect, practicing, 162–63
focus
contribution to greater good and,
49, 50
on others (*See* focusing on others)
focusing on others, 69–97
abuse of power and loss of, 96–97,
101–2, 103–16
empathy and, 8, 72, 73–83
enduring power and, 71–96
experience of power and, 69–71
giving and, 8, 72, 83–86
gratitude and, 8, 72, 87–91
storytelling and, 8, 72–73, 91–96
food sharing, 59–60
Foucault, Michel, 37

Franklin, Ben, 66
friendships, 31

Garner, Eric, 10
Garnett, Kevin, 85–86
Gawker, 66
generosity, 161–62
given by others, power as, 4–7, 41–68
    advance greater good, power is
        given to those who, 5, 43, 44,
        47–54
    gossip as punishment for those
        undermining greater good and,
        43–44, 63–68
    greater good concept and, 44–46
    natural state experiment and,
        41–43
    reputation as determining capacity
        to influence and, 5–6, 43, 44,
        54–59
    status and esteem as reward for
        advancing greater good and,
        6, 43, 44, 59–63
giving, 8, 72, 83–86, 161–62
    empowering others through,
        161–62
    grooming in primates and, 83
    touch and, 83–86
Godfather, The (film), 4
Golding, William, 41–42
goodwill, 90–91
Google, 14
gorillas. *See* primates
gossip, 6, 43–44, 63–68
    abuses of, 63, 66
    behavior that diminishes greater
        good as target of, 64–65
    benefits of allowing, 66–68
    character flaw confirmation and,
        63–64
    flow of, through social networks,
        65–66
    political, 64
    reputation established by, 64
gratitude, 8, 72, 87–91

abuses of power and capacity for,
    101–2, 110
benefits of practicing, 87–88
defined, 87
expressions of, 88–91
food-sharing exchanges and, 88
goodwill generated by, 90–91
grateful mindset exercise, 87–88
Smith on, 87
spoken, 90
ties within social networks, as
    means of building, 89
touch and, 88–89, 90
Gray, Freddie, 10
greater good concept, 44–46
grooming, 83

hard power, 13
Hawthorne, Nathaniel, 54–55
high-empathy individuals,
    performance of, 82
Hitler, Adolf, 21
Holla Back NYC (blog), 66
House of Cards (TV show), 4
HPA axis, 148–49, 155
Huffington, Ariana, 27
Hume, David, 87
humility, 160–61
hunter-gatherer societies, 5
    advance greater good, power given
        to individuals who, 50–51
    context-specific nature of power
        and, 35
Hussein, Saddam, 21
Hutcheson, Francis, 44

impulsivity, 101, 102, 116–28
    eating and, 117–18
    four-way stop study and, 121–24
    right-of-way at crosswalks study
        and, 124–25
    sex and, 118–20
    shoplifting profiles and, 127
    taking candy from children study
        and, 126

threat of, faced by powerless, 145
unethical behavior and, 120–28
wealth and, 121–27
incivility and disrespect, 101, 102,
    128–30
effects of, 129–30
in language and communication,
    128–29
rudeness, incidence of, 129
infidelity, 119–20
Instagram, 14
intellectual function, 152–53
interactions, power as element of. *See*
    relationships and interactions,
    power as element of
IQ testing, 133

Jackson, Andrew, 63
Jackson, Rachel, 63
James, LeBron, 27
James, William, 61
Jefferson, Thomas, 64
Jones, Matt, 80
Jordan, David Starr, 133
Julius Caesar (Shakespeare), 4

kindness, 49, 50
knowledge about world, altering, 25

Lady Gaga, 26
leaderless group discussion
    paradigm, 33–34
life events, explanations of, 132
Limbaugh, Rush, 27
Lincoln, Abraham, 74, 75, 82, 91
listening, 82
Lord of the Flies (Golding), 41–42,
    46, 47

Macbeth (Shakespeare), 4
Machiavelli, Niccolò, 2, 19–20, 99
mana, 69
manufactured items, 27
Mill, John Stuart, 44
mimicry, 106–8

money. *See* wealth
Ms., 128
mutual influence, 29

narratives of exceptionalism.
    See exceptionalism narratives
natural state experiments, 41–43
Netsilik Inuit, 59
New Yorker, The, 37

Obama, Barack, 64
Onion, The, 27, 66
On the Origin of Species
    (Darwin), 36
open-ended questions, 82
openness, 49, 50
opinions
    altering, 26
    of others, soliciting, 83
opposition movements, 20–21
Origins of Totalitarianism, The
    (Arendt), 37
ostracism, 54, 67–68

panic attacks, 153
parent-child relationships, 31–33
patterns, 1
    power paradox (*See* power
        paradox)
perspective taking, 109–10
physical environments, threats posed
    by, 143
physical states, altering, 25–26
politeness, 61
political gossip, 64
political state, altering, 25
Pol Pot, 21
poor health, of powerless, 142,
    154–56
    in children, 155–56
    social class, and vulnerability
        to disease, 140–41, 154–56
    in women, 154–55
poverty, 9–10. *See also* powerless/
    powerlessness

power, 2–7
  coercive force and fraud and, 2–3,
      19–22
  defined, 2–4, 11, 23
  difference in world, as capacity to
      make, 3–4, 23–40
  esteem and, 6
  ethical principles to enduring,
      159–64
  focusing on others and, 69–97
  as given to us by others, 4–7,
      41–68
  Machiavelli's influence on our
      view of, 2
  paradox of (See power paradox)
  principles of, list of, 16–17
  reputation and, 5–6
  rise to, abuse of, and fall from
      pattern (See power paradox)
  science of, 11–15
  as state of mind, 7
powerless/powerlessness, 9–10,
      137–58
  author's childhood experience of,
      138–42, 156–57, 158
  coercive force and, 21
  individual's ability to contribute to
      society undermined by, 141–42,
      151–54
  poor health and, 142, 154–56
  psychological context of,
      changing, 163–64
  social class and vulnerability to
      disease, 140–41
  stress response and, 10, 141, 142,
      146–51
  theories as to causes of,
      139–40
  threat experienced by, 10, 141, 142,
      143–46
  as warning sign of power
      paradox, 136
power paradox, 6–7
  abuses of power (See abuses of
      power)

  balancing of self-gratification and
      focus on others and, 8
  defined, 1–2
  effects of, 2
  feeling or power as beginning of,
      39–40
  powerlessness and (See powerless/
      powerlessness)
  seductions of power and, 9
  transcending, 156–58
  warning signs of, 135–36
preferences, altering, 26
primates, 5
  advance greater good, power given
      to individuals who, 51–54
  context-specific nature of power
      and, 35
  food-sharing exchanges and, 88
  grooming, role of, 83
Prince, The (Machiavelli), 2, 19–20

racism, 10, 143–44
relationships and interactions,
      power as element of, 23, 24,
      27–32
  friendships and, 31
  manufactured items and, 27
  parent-child relationships and,
      31–33
  romantic relationships and,
      30–31
  sibling relations and, 29–30
  social relationships and (See social
      relationships and interactions)
reputation, 5–6, 43, 44, 54–59
  awareness of judgment of others
      and, 56
  gossip as establishing, 64
  intuition and, 56
  opportunity to influence and, 56
  shaming and, 54–56
respect, 162–63
romantic relationships, 30–31
rudeness, 129
Russell, Bertrand, 22

St. Paul, 63

Sassoon, Vidal, 26

Saturday Night Live
(TV show), 27

Scarlet Letter, The (Hawthorne),
54–55

Seward, William, 73–74

sex
dysfunction, and powerlessness,
152
impulsivity and, 118–20

sexual affairs, 119–20

shamemasks (Schandmasken),
55–56, 57

shaming, 55–56

Shittytipper Twitter, The, 66

shoplifting, 127

sibling relations, 29–30

Skellenger, Jerry, 138

Skellenger, Lorraine, 138

slavery, 25, 45

Smith, Adam, 87

Snapchat, 14

Snowden, Edward, 27

social change, altering people's
understanding of world and, 25

social class
capacity for empathy and, 108–9,
111–13
defined, 11–12
disease vulnerability and, 140–41,
154–56
power and, 23

social Darwinism, 133

social hierarchies, biological
explanations for, 134–35

social networks, empowerment
of others in. *See* empowering
others in social networks

social practices for bringing out
good in others, 8

social relationships and interactions
emotional expressions and, 75
empathy and, 73–83
power as element of, 29–33

storytelling and, 91–96
touch and, 83–86

society, powerlessness as impacting
ability to contribute to, 141–42,
151–54
anxiety, vulnerability to, 153
depression, vulnerability
to, 154
intellectual function, impairment
of, 152–53
sexual response, impairment
of, 152

soft power, 13

Stalin, Joseph, 21

states of other people, altering, 23,
24–27
beliefs and, 26–27
economic state and, 24–25
knowledge about world
and, 25
opinions and, 26
physical states and, 25–26
political state and, 25
preferences and, 26
tastes and, 26

status
awards and, 62
behaviors elevating, 61–62
defined, 11
food sharing and, 59–60
as reward for advancing greater
good and, 43, 44, 59–63
without power, 60–61

Steinem, Gloria, 128

Stewart, Jon, 27

Stewart, Martha, 27

storytelling, 8, 72–73, 91–96
conflicts, as providing context for,
94–95
Lincoln's capacity for, 91
stressful challenges and traumas,
as providing sense to, 95
taunting and, 93–94
teasing and, 92–93
by young children, 93–94

stress
  cortisol and, 10, 141, 142, 148–51
  cytokine system and, 148–49
  storytelling and, 95
  threat-induced, experienced by
    powerless, 10, 141, 142,
    146–51
  touch, impact of, 84
  Trier Social Stress Task (TSST)
    and, 146–48
survival-of-the-fittest
  theories, 133

tastes, altering, 26
taunting, 93–94
teasing, 92–93
telomeres, 155
*Theory of Moral Sentiments,
  The* (Smith), 87
threat
  biology of social, 146–51
  children's hypersensitivity to,
    145–46
  continual, faced by powerless,
    10, 141, 142, 143–46
  evolutionary sensitivities to, 143
  of impulsivity of more powerful
    people, 145
  physical environments and, 143
  racism and, 143–44
  stress response to, and effects,
    141, 142, 146–51
  women, violence against,
    144–45

touch
  basketball performance, effect on,
    84–86
  empathy and, 83–86
  gratitude and, 88–89, 90
  stress, impact on, 84
Trier Social Stress Task (TSST),
  146–48
Tumblr, 14
Tutu, Desmond, 38–39, 86
Twitter, 14

Ubuntu, 86
unethical behavior, 120–28
utilitarianism, 44–46

vagus nerve, 113

wealth
  impulsivity and, 121–27
  inequality of, 9–10, 131–32
  power and, 23
Wealth of Nations, The (Smith), 87
Weed, Thurlow, 73–74, 82
Winfrey, Oprah, 27
wisdom, 1
women
  social class, and vulnerability to
    disease, 154–55
  violence against, 144–45

x'iopini, 69

Yelp, 66

Image Credits

Page

28: © The Trustees of the British Museum

32: Courtesy of the author

52: Photogaph by Catherine Marin

53, top: Photograph by Frans de Waal

53, bottom: Photograph by Frans de Waal

79, 1st row, left: Courtesy of Dr. Lenny Kristal

79, 1st row, right: Courtesy of Dr. Lenny Kristal

79, 2nd row, left: Courtesy of Dr. Lenny Kristal

79, 2nd row, right: Courtesy of Dr. Lenny Kristal

79, 3rd row, left: Courtesy of Dr. Lenny Kristal

79, 3rd row, right: Courtesy of Dr. Lenny Kristal

79, 4th row, left: Courtesy of Dr. Lenny Kristal

79, 4th row, right: Courtesy of Dr. Lenny Kristal

81, 1st row, left: Courtesy of Matt Jones

81, 1st row, right: Courtesy of Matt Jones

81, 2nd row, left: Courtesy of Matt Jones

81, 2nd row right: Courtesy of Matt Jones

81, 3rd row, left: Courtesy of Matt Jones

81, 3rd row, right: Courtesy of Matt Jones

81, 4th row, left: Courtesy of Matt Jones

81, 4th row, right: Courtesy of Matt Jones

81, 5th row, left: Courtesy of Matt Jones

81, 5th row, right: Courtesy of Matt Jones